TINY TREASURES

Virginia Enright

A J.B. Fairfax Press Publication

EDITORIAL
MANAGING EDITOR
Judy Poulos

EDITORIAL ASSISTANT
Ella Martin

EDITORIAL COORDINATOR
Margaret Kelly

PHOTOGRAPHY
Richard Weinstein

STYLING
Kathy Tripp

ILLUSTRATION
Lesley Griffith

PRODUCTION AND DESIGN
MANAGER
Anna Maguire

PRODUCTION EDITOR AND LAYOUT
Sheridan Packer

DESIGN MANAGER
Drew Buckmaster

CONCEPT DESIGN
Jenny Pace

PUBLISHED BY J.B. FAIRFAX PRESS PTY LIMITED
80-82 MCLACHLAN AVE
RUSHCUTTERS BAY
AUSTRALIA 2011
A.C.N. 003 738 430

FORMATTED BY J.B. FAIRFAX PRESS PTY LIMITED

PRINTED BY TOPPAN PRINTING CO. SINGAPORE

JBFP 473

TINY TREASURES
ISBN 1 86343 300 7

Acknowledgments

Special thanks to my family: Jim, Claire, Luke and Angela, who saw me through this project.
Without the support and encouragement of my many students and friends, I would not have had the courage to take on this task. Many thanks to all of you.

Virginia

Contents

Introduction

Why make miniature quilts? Make one yourself and you'll know the answer. Once you've started, you'll find many reasons to make mini quilts: the thrill of the colours coming together, the accuracy of your tiny pieces and the speed of finishing a whole quilt. They make wonderful gifts for friends, are great for hanging in small houses and the cost is minimal.

My first miniature quilts were made when the family all had a large quilt on their beds, with a few on the walls and a few more in the cupboards. How many large quilts can you make?

I love the finished miniature quilts, but also take pleasure in choosing the design, the fabrics and the skill in sewing tiny pieces accurately. It's not a process to be rushed – just because it's little, doesn't mean to say the quilt will be run up overnight. Take your time and enjoy yourself.

My father has always shown attention to detail in the work he does. A retired airline pilot, he made prize-winning model planes for a hobby, and also loves to restore antiques. He will patiently spend hours restoring a piece of furniture or gluing a broken piece of china so that it looks as good as new. I feel this attention to detail has rubbed off on me and is now reflected in my work.

When I attended my first patchwork classes, I remember the teacher giving us a general guide as to how difficult a single-bed quilt would be to make: up to 400 pieces for a beginner, 400 to 800 pieces for an intermediate quilter, and over 1000 pieces for advanced students only. Never in my wildest dreams did I ever think that I could make a quilt 12 cm (5 in) square with 370 pieces.

There are many people who can piece accurately, but I can only aspire to this standard. I consider my sewing skills to be average, but with patience and a variety of different techniques, I can sew perfectly too. Regularly teaching patchwork and miniature patchwork classes has improved my awareness of the skills that students need to complete their work. With a little practice and lots of patience, you will master these skills in no time at all. Through this book I hope to share the necessary skills with you, so that you can make your own beautiful tiny treasures.

Teatime

Fabric

Now, this is the best part of quiltmaking, the part we all love, but for some people it's the most stressful part. Over the years, I have been to many colour classes, studied the colour wheel and learnt the rules, but after all that, I feel you should let your heart rule. I encourage everyone to attend classes on colour; the more we know about colour and how to use it the better our work will be. When we first look at any art work it is usually the colours that grab us, then we start to analyse the design, pattern and workmanship. How many times have you looked at a quilt at a show and instinctively hated it, only to reconsider it at a second viewing? Chances are that your first response was an emotional reaction to the colours.

There's not enough room for me to give you an in-depth class on colour here. Instead, I will explain my colour rules the way I present them to a class.

Start with the 'feel' of the quilt. What is the look that you are trying to achieve? Think of the design you have chosen and the different effects that fabrics will have on that design. Look at the 'Red Schoolhouse' quilt on page 71. The colours that I chose for this quilt are traditional for that design. 'Amish Schoolhouses' on page 50 is the same pattern, again worked in plain fabrics, but with a variety of subdued plains on a black background. The Amish quilt is more subtle than the high contrast red and white quilt. Imagine the same block worked in soft pastel print fabrics – your quilt would have a very different look to the two quilts pictured in this book.

After you have chosen a design, choose the appropriate fabrics to achieve that look:

- country – choose checks, stars and darker prints;
- Amish – black and plain fabrics;
- pastel – soft florals, pastel checks and pastel plains;
- Christmas – reds, greens, perhaps black and gold; or
- contemporary – bold prints and plains.

I am fortunate to have a large scrap bag to work from. Since I don't have a studio, I wait till all the family is out, then turn the bag out on the lounge room floor and sort the fabric into different piles.

For a country-style quilt, I would sort out all the checks, plaids, stripes and plains that could be suitable. These fabrics are then laid out in an overlapping row on a white background, such as a white sheet or pillowcase, as other colours can be distracting.

When they are laid out, look at the fabrics again through the viewfinder of a camera, or through a door peephole (available at your local hardware store). This clarifies the range of fabrics and some colours will jump out at you.

Next, I decide on the colours I want to use. Often, I let the fabrics tell me what colour the quilt will be. If the majority of fabrics are burgundy, I will make a burgundy quilt rather than rush out and buy new blue fabric. My mother instilled in me the 'make do' instinct!

Included in that row of fabrics could be lights and darks, greens, reds, blues, tans and black. Play around with the fabrics and you will be surprised at the different looks that you can achieve. For example, take out all the dark colours. Is this palette too light? If so, put a few dark colours back.

Take out all the blues. Is this too 'Christmassy' with mainly red and green? Or take out all the light colours and work with a very dark, subtle palette.

When you have decided on the fabrics that you like, put all the remaining colours away and work with just the ones you have chosen. This saves confusion later on.

You may like to look back to the design and make definite choices for the blocks, but I prefer to make the decisions as I go. I would make up a block, then choose the fabrics for the next block as I go. This may seem rather free and easy for you, however miniature quiltmaking should be a learning experience. As you are not involved with large expensive pieces of fabric, I challenge you to go outside your normal boundaries and experiment a little.

VARIETY AND SCALE

Study all the quilts in this book and you will notice that quite often I will use a large variety of fabrics in one quilt. The easiest fabrics to work with are tone-on-tone fabrics – a fabric in one colour with a similar-coloured overall print. They add interest to your work without the problems of high-contrast fabrics. High-contrast fabrics, for example, a blue background with an all-over white floral print, can upset the overall design of your work. If you have a white background fabric next to the blue-and-white fabric, from a distance the seam line will bleed from one side to the other. If it were a tone-on-tone blue next to a white background, there would be a sharp contrast and the pieces in the block would be more clearly defined.

Include a variety of different-sized prints in your work. Miniature quilts invite us to look closely at them, so a variety of prints creates interest across the surface of the quilt and your eye will roam from one section to the other.

Upon completion of the quilt you may decide that the whole piece looks too busy. Choose a plain fabric for the inner border and you'll be pleased with the effect. The narrow border of plain fabric gives your eyes somewhere to rest and balances the rest of the work.

CONTRAST

This can make or break your quilt. Any piecing in a quilt that you want to define needs to have a high contrast between the piecing in the block and the background. White or beige backgrounds work best, clearly allowing the pieced section of the block to dominate. When the quilt hangs on the wall and is viewed from a distance, it would be a shame for all the pieces to blend together, looking just like another piece of fabric.

Contrast is important in the 'Tumbling Blocks' quilt (page 62) for the design to be easily recognised. Originally, I started with light, medium and dark fabrics, but the definition was very subtle and the pattern was lost. By changing to a light and medium palette, with all beige fabrics for the third choice, the pattern became clear.

Compare the contrast in the 'Red Schoolhouse' quilt (page 71) and the 'Amish Schoolhouses' quilt (page 50). The Amish quilt is very subtle with one of the houses nearly disappearing in the corner. On the other hand, the Red Schoolhouse quilt has a high contrast between the fabrics. This makes it very unforgiving, if there are any mistakes.

Tone-on-tone beige fabrics are my favourites for backgrounds. For most work, there is usually enough contrast between the beige fabric and the other fabrics in the block. They also add interest to the block. However, if you are working with blocks that are only 4 cm (1 1/2 in), plain beige gives a clearer look.

Detail of the Pineapple quilt on page 48

Skills

Throughout the book, measurements are given in metric with the imperial measurements following in brackets. These are not exact equivalents. It does not matter which system of measurements you use, but you mustn't change from one to the other.

SEAM ALLOWANCE

All my students tell me that their sewing machines can sew an accurate 6 mm (1/4 in) seam allowance, but it is surprising the number of machines that sew a little bit under or a little bit over on a test sample. On a large quilt, this little bit may be taken up in the seams and even itself out, but imagine a 5 cm (2 in) block with four seams across it. All those little bits could add up to 1 cm (3/8 in), which is a lot to try and fudge.

I suggest you do a sample, before you start sewing any seams. It only takes a minute to do and the results may surprise you. Cut three strips of fabric, each 32 mm x 8 cm (1 1/2 in x 3 in). Sew them together as shown in figure 1. The centre strip should be 2 cm (1 in) wide.

Be aware that it is possible to run the seam line off at the end so that it is narrower than 6 mm (1/4 in). If you find yourself doing this, use the unpicker as a guide to hold the fabric firmly while you sew.

Work with an accurate 6 mm (1/4 in) seam allowance and trim it back to a scant 3 mm (1/8 in) if the seam is too bulky. If you are familiar with working with the 6 mm (1/4 in) seam allowance, you can quickly tell if you are accurate or not.

Sewing Guide

Many machines have presser feet where the needle is exactly 6 mm (1/4 in) from the edge of the foot. This allows you to run your fabric along the edge of the foot and guarantee that the seam will be accurate.

If you are having trouble with your seam allowance, this technique may help you. Take a piece of graph paper (metric or imperial) and cut along a line on the paper. From that cut edge, mark the width of the seam. Place the drawn seam line under the needle. The edge of the paper will be 6 mm (1/4 in) from the needle. Lay a strip of mounting tape or corn-pad plaster along the edge of the paper. This tape or plaster is ideal to use as it is thicker than normal tape and gives you a ridge to run your fabric along.

Make up another sample before sewing to check that the marker is in the correct position.

PRESSING

Bumpy seam allowances can be a pest and must be eliminated. When piecing a block, try to press the seams in opposite directions to distribute the bulk in one area. When a block has been sewn together, it may be necessary to press some of the seams open to keep the work flat.

Always use a small pressing cloth on your work. As there are so many bumpy seams in a small area, it is easy for your work to end up with a shine, if you press without a cloth.

Be gentle when pressing your work. Please don't be aggressive and iron indiscriminately. This is a small piece of work; be gentle with it.

Students often bring their first finished block to show me and I am horrified at the way they try to pull it into shape. The block may not be absolutely perfect, but when sewn to the next block many of the problems will, hopefully, disappear. If you have tried to pull the block into shape, the problems may only become worse.

STITCH LENGTH

There is no hard-and-fast rule on stitch length. My rule is: the shorter the seam, the shorter the stitch length. Some seams may be 6 mm (1/4 in) and would need tiny stitches, but for a 5 cm (2 in) seam, four stitches to the centimetre (or to 3/8 in) would be suitable.

NEEDLE DOWN

If you have the needle-down facility on your machine, please use it. The tiny pieces of fabric tend to jump around when you stop sewing, but if you use the needle-down facility, it's just like having an extra pair of hands.

SEWING SPEED

It may be obvious to some of you, but please slow down when you are sewing seams that are only 2.5 cm (1 in) long. I am surprised at the speed at which some people tackle their work. Perhaps they are used to production-line work, not fine, delicate stitching. Hold your work firmly, sew slowly and you'll be pleased with the results.

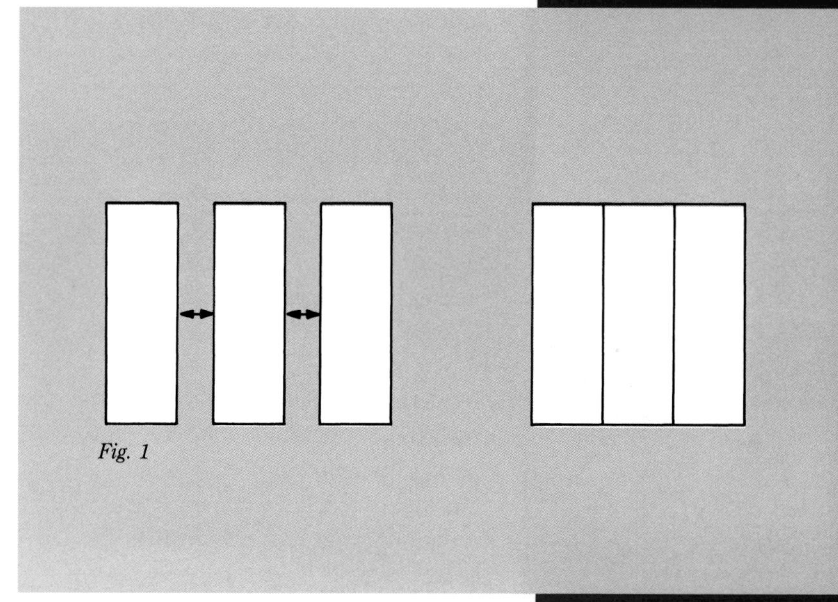

Fig. 1

Techniques

HAND-PIECING AND TEMPLATES

Some of the quilts in the book are hand-pieced and it is necessary to make templates. Trace the pattern onto the template plastic with a sharp pencil or marking pen, include the grain-line markings and the number of the pattern piece, then cut it out. Check the finished template with the original pattern to see that it is correct.

All the templates are given as the finished size of the piece, so seam allowances need to be added. If you are working with metric measurements, it is suggested you add 6 mm, and add 1/4 in for imperial measurements. Lay the template onto the wrong side of the fabric and trace round it with a sharp pencil. A piece of fine sandpaper placed under the fabric holds it firmly while you do this.

Cut out the fabrics, lining up your template with the grain-line markings and remembering to add the seam allowances. Store all the cut fabrics in small plastic bags.

Joining Patches

Select the pieces to be sewn together. Place a pin at the end of the seam line through both points. Start to sew at the other end of the row with a small back stitch. Check the back of your work as you sew to see that you are still on the line.

FOUNDATION PIECING

Foundation piecing, where tiny pieces are sewn not to each other alone but to a base or foundation, enables us to sew tiny blocks accurately. Most of the quilts in this book are constructed with this method. It is a similar technique to crazy patchwork, but with a formal pattern instead of random scraps.

The patterns in this book are given without any seam allowances. Seam allowances are added to the outer edges of the block.

Begin by tracing the pattern onto firm white paper. This way you can reuse the pattern many times without damaging the book. Tape the tracing to a firm surface with the interfacing over it. I prefer to use medium-weight interfacing and leave it in the finished piece of work. Paper is difficult to pick out of the finished piece and calico is not as firm to work on as the interfacing.

Your finished piece is only as accurate as your original tracing, so take your time, use a sharp pencil and be accurate. Include all the numbers when tracing onto the interfacing as they indicate the sequence of sewing (Detail 1).

Piecing on Foundation

Roughly cut the fabric to the correct size, adding a seam allowance and a little bit more. I like to cut the fabrics on the generous side as it can be frustrating to sew a piece on, flip it back, then find it is too short.

Start with the centre of the block – usually piece 1. Lay the first fabric on the unmarked side of the interfacing with the right side out (Detail 2). Hold the interfacing up to the light to see if you have covered the necessary area and allowed a 6 mm (1/4 in) seam allowance. Lay the next fabric over the first one with the right sides together (Detail 3). Turn the foundation over and sew on the drawn line between pieces 1 and 2, starting three stitches before the line and finishing three stitches after the line (Detail 4). Trim the seam allowance, then flip the top fabric out (Detail 5).

Small blocks need to be pressed as you go for best results. Set the iron up beside your machine so you can sew and iron as you go.

Lay the next fabric down with the right sides together on the previous piece and continue in the same manner: sew, trim and press till the section or strip is completed (Detail 6). Press the finished piece and trim, leaving a 6 mm (1/4 in) seam allowance

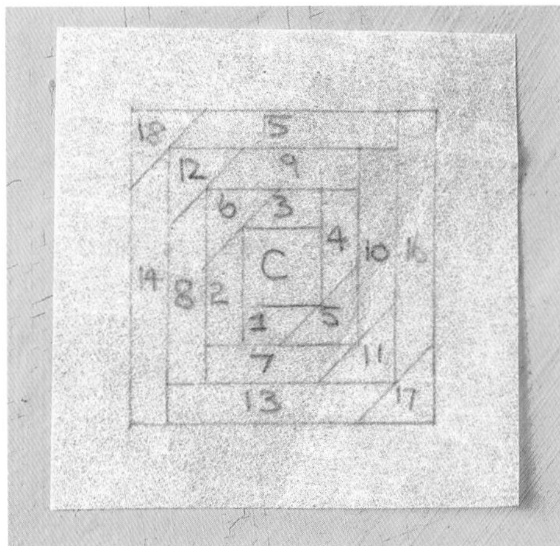

Detail 1: Trace onto interfacing

Detail 2: Position piece 1

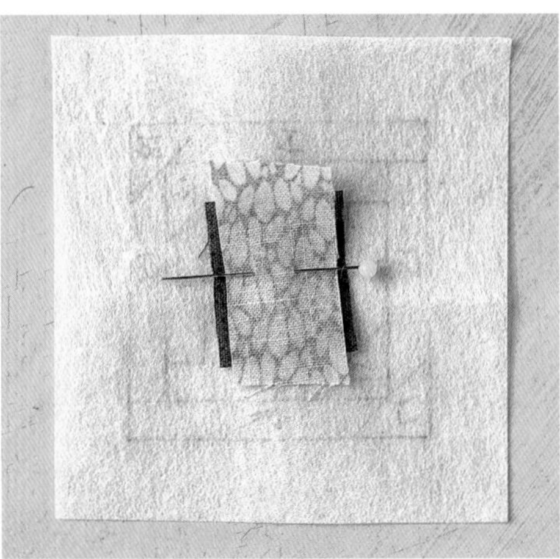

Detail 3: Position piece 2

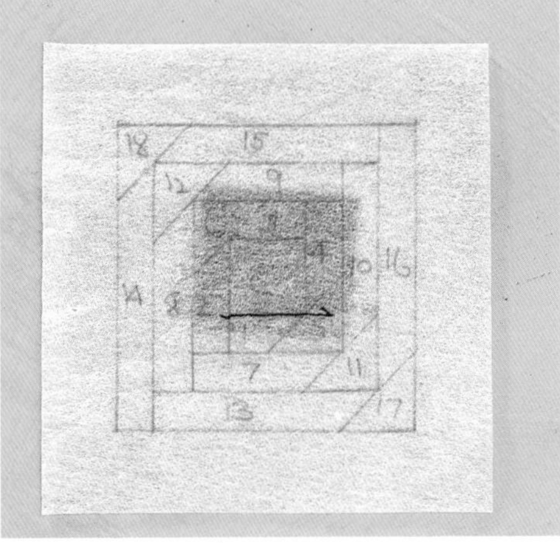

Detail 4: Sew the first seam

round the edge of the block (Detail 7). Turn the piece over and you have the finished block (Detail 8).

When sewing the finished sections together, sew with a large stitch, check that all the necessary points meet, then oversew with a smaller stitch. Invariably one point doesn't meet the first time, so it is better to take the precaution of sewing with a large stitch first than trying to undo a tiny stitch.

When sewing foundations to sashing strips or borders, sew with the foundation uppermost. This way you will have the line on the foundation to use as a guide for accurate sewing.

COMPLETING A QUILT

Mitring Borders

Cut the borders to the individual measurements given in each project. Sew the narrow inner border to the outer border and press the seam towards the outer border.

If length measurements are not given, measure through the centre of the quilt for the correct measurement (Fig. 1). Pin the borders to the quilt, allowing enough fabric for the borders to overlap. Start and finish the sewing 6 mm (1/4 in) from the edge of the quilt (Fig. 2).

Lay the quilt on a firm surface with the borders sitting flat. Fold the top border at an angle of 45 degrees to the side border and pin (Fig. 3). Use a quilter's ruler to check that the angle is correct. With small quilts I prefer to slipstitch the seam, which enables you to line the inner border up correctly. Finish the other corners in the same manner.

Assembling a Quilt

There is a variety of different waddings available. Use one that is thin with a low

Detail 5: Flip piece 2 back

Detail 6: Continue pieceing the block

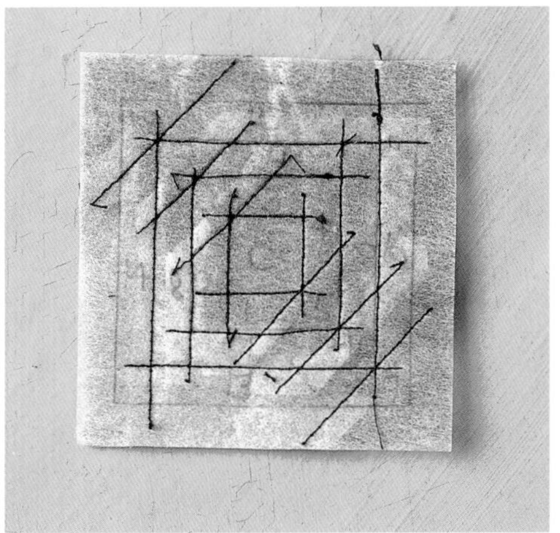

Detail 7: Trim the block

Detail 8: The completed block

loft. Those that are too thick prevent the quilt from draping well and are difficult to quilt with tiny stitches. Pellon and 80 per cent cotton/20 per cent polyester types are suitable.

Choose a suitable backing fabric for the quilt, be it pieced leftovers or fabric that coordinates with the quilt top. I like to use a picture print fabric – those whimsical fabrics that we buy because we love them, but then find them difficult to work with.

Lay the backing fabric down right side down, lay the wadding on top, then the quilt front on top, with the right side up. I like to gently press the three layers together and slightly block the quilt to the wadding. This is a technique that I only use with small quilts, but it helps the layers to sit well together, without any puckers. Pin the quilt, then baste the layers together with a needle and thread. Safety pins are usually too large for small work and can move the work slightly when pinning.

Quilting

Hand-quilting can be difficult on a small quilt, if your stitches are too large. Most designs are machine-quilted in the ditch, which is enough to hold the design together and overcomes the problem of too-large stitches. Be careful when quilting in small blocks that the quilting doesn't distort your work.

The quilting design can be marked onto the quilt top with a lead pencil, lightly, or a washable marking pen. Test the marking pen first on a piece of fabric for suitability. Fancy designs, such as hearts, can be cut from Contact paper, then stuck on the quilt wherever needed. Quilt round, then remove them. This is an easy way of working, without the worry of marking lines showing on your finished work. Masking tape can be used for marking straight-line quilting in the same way as the Contact paper is used for marking fancy designs.

Heavy quilting is best shown in the outer borders. Choose a plain or tone-on-tone fabric, if you plan to quilt the borders heavily so the quilting design will be highlighted. Quilting tends to blend in on print fabrics.

Trim the wadding and backing fabric when the quilting is finished. Check that the corners are square and the same width at the top and bottom. Quilts are usually hung on a light-coloured wall, which shows up any size difference.

Binding

Cut a strip of fabric 4.5 cm (1 3/4 in) wide on the straight grain of the fabric. You may need to join strips if your fabric is too short. Do this with a diagonal seam (Figs 4, 5 and 6).

If you have a seam in the binding, lay the binding onto the quilt before sewing and check where the binding seam will be. I start the binding near the bottom right-hand corner and try to have a join at the top left-hand corner. This way the binding seams are in a balanced position and you don't end up with all the binding seams on one side of the quilt.

Cut the end of the binding on the diagonal and press a small allowance under (Fig. 7). Fold the binding strip in half, lengthwise, with the wrong sides together and press. Lay the binding on the quilt at or near the bottom right-hand corner of the quilt (Fig. 8). Start stitching 5 cm (2 in) from the end of the binding and sew with a 6 mm (1/4 in) seam to 6 mm (1/4 in) from the end of the quilt. Fold the binding at an angle of 45 degrees to the top of the quilt, then fold it back down along the edge of the quilt (Figs 9 and 10). Start stitching from the edge of the quilt and sew the remaining binding in the same manner.

To join the ends of the binding, lay the end of the binding inside the start of the binding and sew over the join. Fold the binding to the back of the quilt and slipstitch the edge in place.

Labelling

In our hurry to finish our work, many times the label is overlooked as being unimportant. Take the time to name and date your work with an embroidered or permanently marked label. Your great-grandchildren will thank you for it one day.

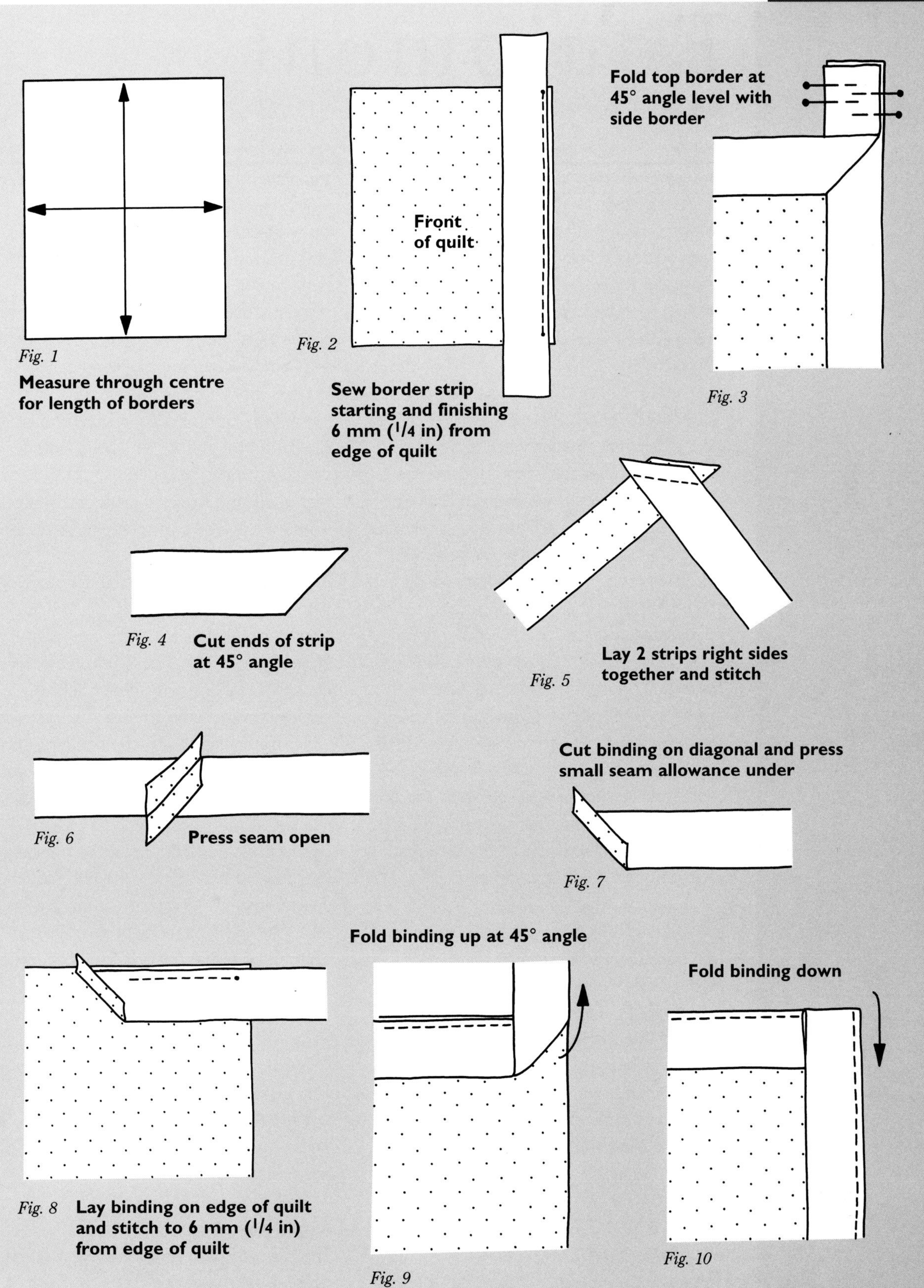

Fig. 1 Measure through centre for length of borders

Fig. 2 Sew border strip starting and finishing 6 mm (1/4 in) from edge of quilt

Fig. 3

Fig. 4 Cut ends of strip at 45° angle

Fig. 5 Lay 2 strips right sides together and stitch

Fig. 6 Press seam open

Fig. 7 Cut binding on diagonal and press small seam allowance under

Fig. 8 Lay binding on edge of quilt and stitch to 6 mm (1/4 in) from edge of quilt

Fig. 9

Fig. 10

Equipment

A tradesman never blames his tools for poor workmanship, but a quilter has my permission to blame poor work on poor tools. Without sharp scissors, a well-serviced machine and a small ruler for rotary cutting, it is difficult to achieve good results in your work. Treat yourself to new equipment regularly; you deserve it.

SEWING MACHINE

As a patchwork teacher who has taught many classes over the years, I have come across many varieties of sewing machines – new machines, old machines, good machines and bad machines. Old machines are not necessarily bad machines – a basic straight-stitch old machine can run rings round some of the latest models. You will know which category yours fall into. For miniature quiltmaking, you will need a machine that sews a straight stitch with an accurate 6 mm (1/4 in) seam allowance.

A flat bed on the machine is also useful. Most machines have a free arm and the flat bed is an attachment that fits round the free arm. This helps to lay the fabric flat before sliding it under the presser foot.

A machine that has a knee bar to lift the presser foot is most helpful with tiny work, as it allows you to have both hands free to align the work under the needle.

I prefer to work with a size 80 needle. If you find that the fabric is being 'chewed up' by the machine, try working with a size 70 needle. Change your needle after every eight hours of sewing time. A needle becomes blunt with use and has trouble piercing the fabric.

ROTARY CUTTERS, RULER AND CUTTING MATS

The advent of the rotary cutter has made an immense difference to quiltmaking. Instead of making templates, drawing round each template and individually cutting the pieces, we can now stack the fabric and cut many pieces at once. The rotary cutter also enables you to be more accurate in your cutting.

In my miniature work, I use the rotary cutter mainly for cutting strips, trimming the edges of foundation pieces and cutting borders and bindings.

Rotary cutters come in small and large sizes and both work well. When cutting with the rotary cutter you need to place a special mat under the fabric to protect the table. These are available at specialist patchwork shops and fabric shops.

Special rulers are available for working with the cutter and mat. The rulers come in a variety of shapes and sizes with metric and imperial measurements. One ruler is never enough. I manage with three rulers. My students often come to class with very long wide rulers which I find cumbersome and awkward when trying to cut tiny amounts of fabric. A 15 cm x 35 cm (6 in x 14 in) size is good for most cutting. A 15 cm (6 in) square is essential. Buy one – remember you deserve it. Look for one that has fine measurements – 3 mm (1/8 in) as well as 2.5 cm (1 in). A number of my students have told me that they prefer this ruler for all their cutting as it is easy to handle.

An optional ruler is a large 30 cm (12 in) square. This size is handy for squaring up the finished quilt top.

OTHER ESSENTIALS

There is a variety of readily available products that you will also need.

Appliqué Foot

This special foot for your sewing machine is open at the front with no bar across it. It is wonderful, as it enables you to see exactly where the needle is entering the fabric.

When you are sewing tiny seams if you're two threads out, you can be in trouble. This foot takes the guesswork out of where you are sewing.

Masking Tape

For taping patterns and interfacing to the table when tracing. Masking tape can also be used as a guide for quilting straight lines.

Unpicker

Students laugh when they see this on my requirements lists, but you will become an expert at using it. Your friends will be quick to point out any mistakes in your quilt so take the time to correct your work as you go, or it will annoy you forever. When working with very tiny pieces, you may find it difficult to unpick. If this is the case, be prepared to throw out the section and start again. Small pieces of fabric can only take so much sewing before they become misshapen. The unpicker can also be used when guiding your work under the machine. If the pieces are too small to hold gently in your fingers, guide them through with the unpicker.

Scissors

Large sharp scissors are necessary for trimming seams and cutting fabric. Small scissors are also useful for cutting threads. Try to keep your work neat as you go. With so many seams in a small area, the back of your work can become a mass of threads if they are not trimmed.

Markers

A variety of markers are also needed. Sharp pencils are needed when tracing the patterns onto the interfacing for foundation work. Choose a hard lead; a soft lead can smudge as you work, giving a grubby look to the finished piece.

To mark quilting designs on your quilt, a washable marker or a chalk marker work well. Remember to test the washable marker on scrap fabrics prior to drawing on your finished work.

Spray Starch

An essential item if you have any fabric that is soft and limp. Spray the fabric that you are working with, prior to cutting out and it will become firmer and easier to handle. I prefer to work with fabric that is not washed and has the sizing left in. If you have already prewashed your fabric, spraying it with the spray starch gives back the body that has been washed out.

Interfacing

Most of the quilts in this book are worked on a foundation. This is similar to making a crazy patchwork, but instead of sewing fabrics on the foundation in a random manner, a pattern is followed. Originally I sewed onto paper onto which I had photocopied the pattern. This was a quick way to work, but removing the paper was a tedious process. Now, I trace the pattern onto the interfacing which is not removed and will be left in place when the quilt is completed.

Medium-weight sew-in interfacing is suitable to use. Iron-on interfacing is unsuitable as you are prevented from ironing the interfacing as you work. Medium-weight is firm enough to support your work as you sew, while fine interfacing is too flimsy and heavyweight too stiff.

Photocopier

A photocopier is useful for copying patterns. In this book I suggest that you photocopy patterns from the book to use as your master copy for tracing. This will enable you to use the pattern many times without the pattern becoming tattered or damaging the book with repeated tracing.

The patterns that are in the book can be enlarged or reduced on a photocopier to the size that suits you. Check that the final block is the required size and is still square and you will have no problems. Some older photocopiers may distort your copy slightly so check your copy before using it.

The Projects

When I think of miniature quilts, I am confronted with an endless list of possibilities in style and technique. Choosing which quilts to make for this book became a difficult choice. I have tried to include something for everyone – from the beginner to the more advanced quilter.

Beginners may like to start with 'Baby Mist' on page 41 or 'Friendship Braid' on page 18. Both quilts use the foundation-piecing technique, but both are quick and simple to sew. You'll be pleased with the results, and I hope you will be inspired to try making some of the other quilts in the book. Be sure to try 'Tumbling Blocks' on page 62 and don't be intimidated by the tiny points in 'Feathered Star and Houses' on page 22 .

All the quilts can be given a new look with a change of colour or fabric. 'Snail's Trail' on page 74 and 'Amish Schoolhouses' on page 50 take on a traditional look, if they are made in country-style fabrics. 'Liberty Baskets' on page 35 can look quite Amish when sewn in a variety of plain fabrics on a black background. I've seen many students start with a simple pattern, and in no time they are exploring different fabrics, colour choices and block sizes, creating quilts in their own style.

Enjoy making your tiny treasures!

Friendship Braid

YOU WILL NEED

For the quilt with the blue border

- **a large variety of small scraps in light and medium range, or all medium range**
- **20 cm (8 in) of gold fabric for the sashing strips**
- **30 cm (12 in) of blue fabric for the outer border**

For the quilt with the green border

- **a large variety of small floral print scraps in lights and darks**
- **10 cm (4 in) of burgundy fabric for the inner border**
- **a large variety of small 30 cm (8 in) of green fabric for the outer border and binding**

For both quilts

- **10 cm (4 in) of medium-weight interfacing**
- **35 cm x 40 cm (14 in x 16 in) of wadding**
- **35 cm x 40 cm (14 in x 16 in) of fabric for the backing**
- **sewing machine**
- **usual sewing supplies**
- **sewing threads to blend with the fabrics**
- **rotary cutter and mat (optional)**
- **quilter's ruler (optional)**
- **masking tape**
- **firm white paper**
- **fineline marker pen**
- **sharp pencil**
- **pressing cloth**

Everyone loves these little treasures. There's something about scrap quilts that makes us look closely at the different fabrics and ask: Have I used any of the same fabrics? Do I have them in my cupboard? Are they the ones I used in my friendship quilt?

The quilt with the green border uses a palette of very dark and very light fabrics. The middle range of fabrics has been eliminated, which establishes a high level of contrast and creates the overall design. The fabric for the quilt with the blue border was given to me by a close friend after she had taken my class in the large Friendship Braid quilt. The quilt was beautiful in the larger size, but when I laid out the strips for the miniature there was no definition anywhere and the fabrics seemed to run into each other. I added the gold sashing strips, and the pattern once again emerged.

Machine-pieced on foundation and machine-quilted

Finished size: quilt with the blue border, 29 cm x 34 cm (11 1/2 in x 13 1/2 in); quilt with the green border, 28 cm x 30 cm (11 in x 12 in)

INSTRUCTIONS

See the Pattern on page 21.

1 Photocopy or trace the pattern onto the firm paper with the marker pen. Use this as your master copy. This allows you to use the pattern repeatedly without damaging your book.

2 Tape the pattern onto a firm surface, then tape the interfacing over the top and trace the pattern onto the interfacing, using the sharp pencil. Include the numbers; they indicate the order of sewing. Shade the interfacing to indicate the dark side. Note that the strips will be reversed when they are sewn.

For the quilt with the green border

1 Trace two copies of row 1 and two copies of row 2.

2 Sort the fabrics into lights and darks. Cut the fabric into strips roughly 2.5 cm (1 in) wide. Starting with piece 1, lay a dark fabric on the back of the interfacing with the right side up, covering position 1 and allowing a 6 mm (1/4 in) seam allowance. Hold the interfacing up to the light and check that the piece is in the correct position. Lay piece 2 (light fabric) over piece 1 with the right sides together and sew along the drawn line between 1 and 2, starting three stitches before the line and finishing three stitches after it. This allows for the seam allowance. Carefully trim the seam, if necessary, and flip piece 2 fabric over. Press.

3 Lay piece 3 down and sew, trim, flip and press, as before. Continue in this manner, alternating the light and dark fabrics. Keep working in this manner till the foundation is completely covered. Press, then trim the edges allowing a 6 mm (1/4 in) seam allowance on all sides of the strip.

4 Complete the remaining strips in the same manner.

For the quilt with the blue border

Trace two copies of row 1 and one copy of row 2. Continue as for the quilt with the green border, using only medium fabrics.

Above: Quilt with the green border
Right: Detail of the quilt above

TO FINISH

For the quilt with the green border

1 Lay the four strips out in the order you wish to sew them. Sew the strips together with a large stitch first. Check that the seams are matching, then oversew them with a smaller stitch.

2 Cut four 2.5 cm (1 in) wide strips for the inner border and four 6 cm (2 1/2 in) wide strips for the outer border. Sew them to the quilt following the instructions for mitred borders on page 11.

For the quilt with the blue border

1 Cut two 2.5 cm (1 in) wide strips of gold fabric the length of the foundation. Sew the sashing between the strips. The foundation should be on top when you are sewing to enable you to see the sewing line.

2 Cut four 2.5 cm (1 in) wide strips for the inner border and four 8 cm (3 1/4 in) wide strips for the outer border. Sew them to the quilt following the instructions for mitred borders on page 11.

For both quilts

1 Lay the backing fabric face down with the wadding on top and the quilt top on top of that, face upwards. Baste the three layers together.

2 Machine-quilt in the ditch around the sashing and borders.

3 Bind and label your quilt.

Quilt with Green Border

Quilt with Blue Border

Detail of the quilt with the blue border

Feathered Star and Houses

YOU WILL NEED

- 30 cm (12 in) of main fabric for the star
- 20 cm (8 in) of fabric for the star points (this can be the same as the star fabric)
- small amount of fabric for the houses
- 40 cm (16 in) of fabric for the background
- 20 cm (8 in) of fabric for the inner border
- 60 cm (24 in) of fabric for the outer border and binding
- 70 cm (28 in) of fabric for the backing
- 70 cm (28 in) of wadding
- 30 cm (12 in) of medium-weight interfacing
- sewing machine
- rotary cutter and mat
- quilter's ruler
- usual sewing supplies
- sewing threads to blend with the fabrics
- quilting thread
- firm white paper
- sharp pencil
- template plastic
- fineline marker pen
- masking tape
- pressing cloth

At one time in our lives we all admire the fine points around a feathered star and aim to make a quilt in this pattern, or at least one block for a wallhanging. Unfortunately these points are quite difficult for the average quilter and one or two lost points seem to spoil the whole effect.

I used the foundation-piecing technique for the houses and the star points. Without it, I wouldn't attempt to tackle this pattern as my points would be far from perfect.

Originally, I was teaching this quilt using rotary cutting techniques. I heard that in an upcoming class I would have a student with multiple sclerosis, so to help her out I thought it would be easier for her to make the quilt using the foundation technique. At the end of the day, she had completed more pieces more accurately than anyone else and they were asking why they couldn't use the foundation method too. The moral of the story is that I now teach this quilt using the foundation technique and achieve much better results.

The finished quilt will have some sections that will have interfacing behind them and other sections that are just fabric.

Machine-pieced on foundation, hand-quilted
Finished size: 62 cm (24 1/2 in) square
Block size: 7.5 cm (3 in)

INSTRUCTIONS

See Pattern and Templates on pages 24-26.

1. Photocopy or trace the pattern onto the firm paper with the marker pen. Use this as your master copy. This allows you to use the pattern repeatedly without damaging your book.
2. Make templates of pieces A, B, C and D.

For the House blocks

1. The House block is made in three segments, then joined together. Tape the pattern to a firm surface and place the interfacing on top. Trace four houses onto the interfacing, leaving room between the segments for 6 mm (1/4 in) seam allowances. Include the numbers as they indicate the sequence of sewing.
2. Piece each segment of the House blocks, following the general instructions for foundation piecing on page 9.
3. Press the finished segments of each block. Trim each segment with the rotary cutter allowing 6 mm (1 1/4 in) seam allowances on all sides of the block.
4. Sew the segments together with a large stitch, check for accuracy, then oversew with a small stitch. If the seams are bulky press them open rather than pressing them to one side.
5. Using template A, cut out five squares from the main star fabric. Lay the squares and houses out for the centre of the quilt in three rows of three. Join the squares and House blocks into rows, then join the rows together (Fig. 1).

For the Star block

1. Trace eight copies of each point segment pattern onto the interfacing.
2. Piece the star point segments, following the general instructions for foundation piecing on page 9. Press the segments, then trim each segment with the rotary cutter allowing 6 mm (1/4 in) seam allowances on all sides.
3. Cut eight triangles from the main star fabric, using template B (adding seam

Detail of the star point

allowances). Sew the star point segments to the B triangles as shown in figure 2.

4 Cut the background fabric using templates C and D (adding seam allowances). Sew the pieced star sections to the background pieces in the sequence shown in figure 3.

5 Sew the elements into three rows, then sew the rows together to form the centre of the quilt top.

TO FINISH

1 Cut four inner borders 4 cm x 71 cm (1 1/2 in x 28 in). Cut the four outer borders 11.5 cm x 71 cm (4 1/2 in x 28 in). Sew them together, then press the seam towards the wide border. Attach the borders to the quilt front, following the general instructions for mitred borders on page 11.

2 Lay the backing fabric face down with the wadding on top and the quilt front on top of that, face upwards. Pin and baste the three layers together.

3 Quilt the background and any other areas you wish with a diagonal grid.

4 Bind and label your quilt.

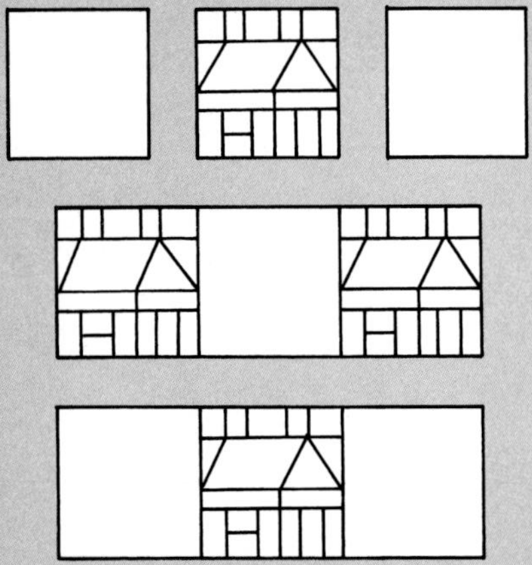

Fig. 1

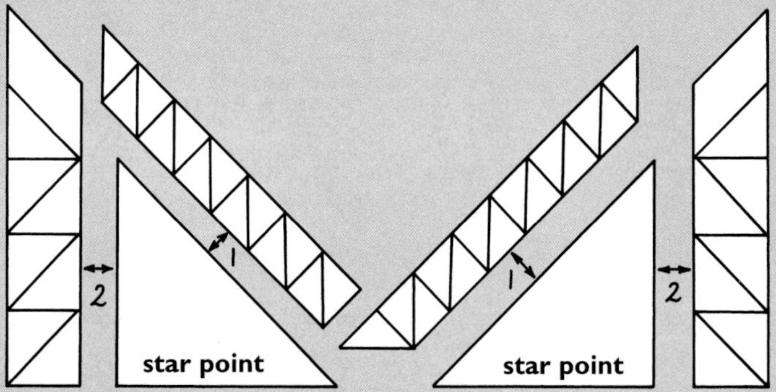

star point

star point

Fig. 2

D

C

D

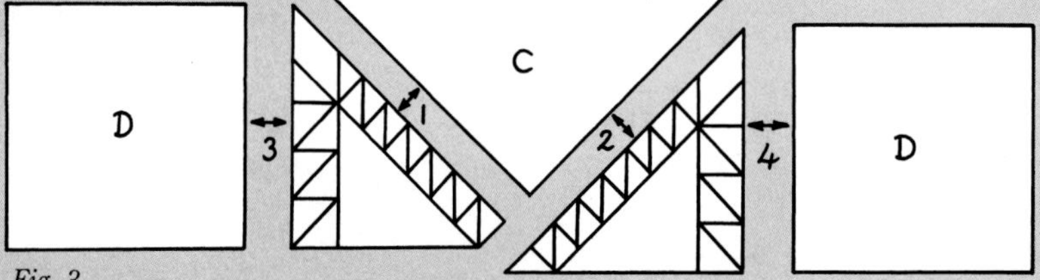

Fig. 3

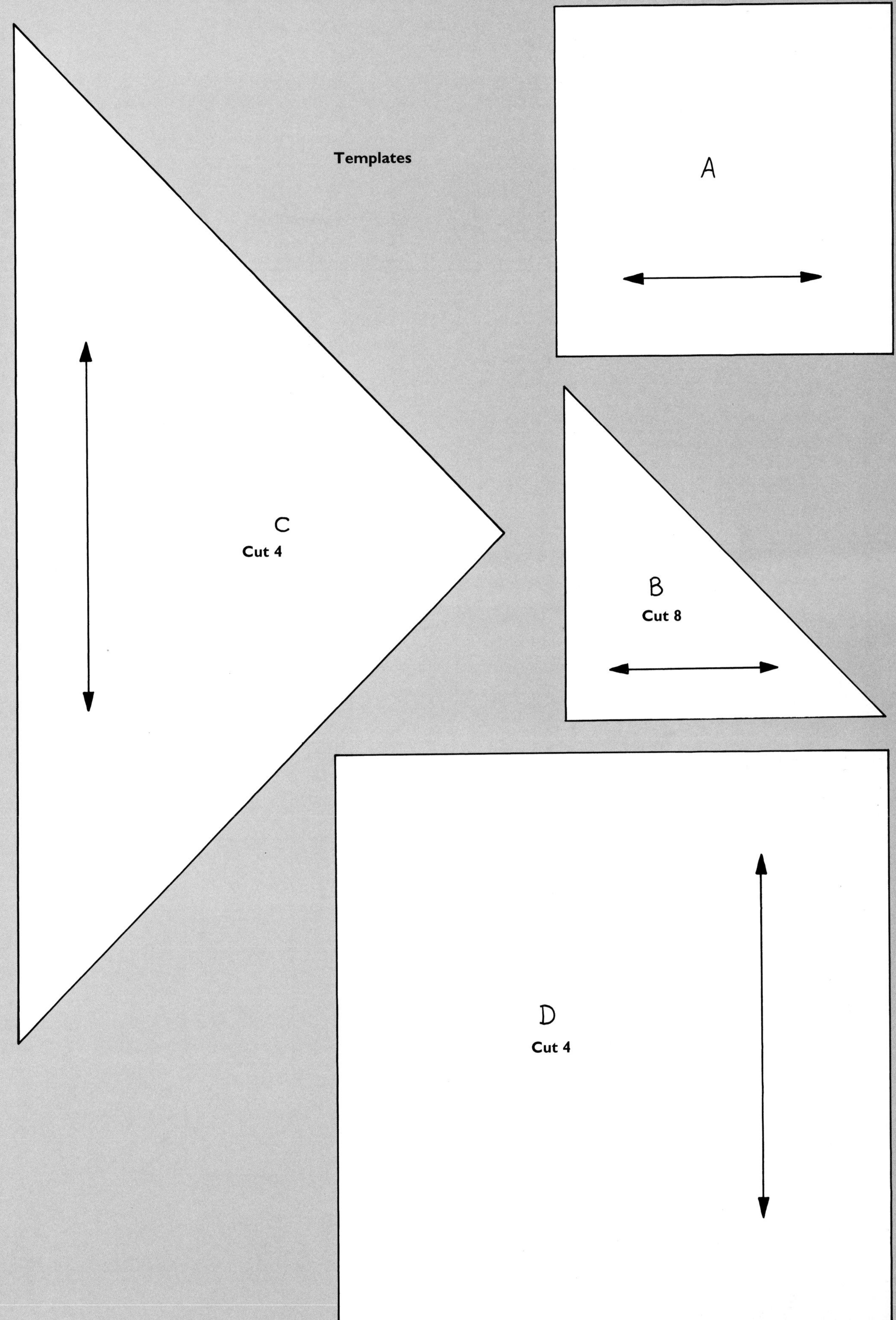
Templates
A
C
Cut 4
B
Cut 8
D
Cut 4

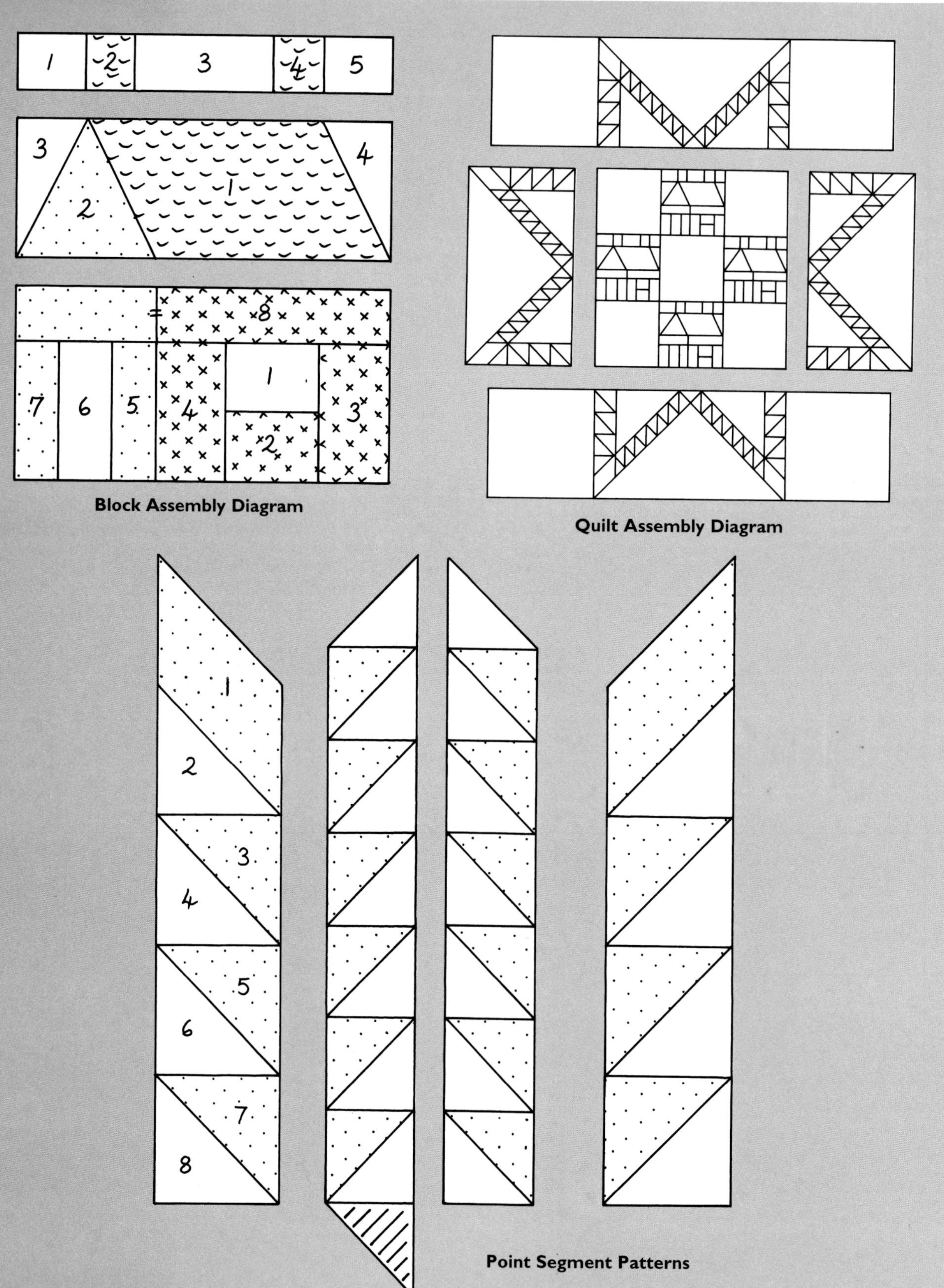

Block Assembly Diagram

Quilt Assembly Diagram

Point Segment Patterns

Celebrate 111

Celebrate 111 is a contemporary alternative to a traditional favourite. The 'geese' at the top of the quilt have been randomly appliquéd and enhanced with beading. The 'flying geese' represent the bubbles flying from a champagne bottle at one of the many celebrations in our lives.

Machine-pieced on foundation and machine-quilted

Finished size: 28 cm x 33 cm (11 in x 13 in)

INSTRUCTIONS

See the Pattern on page 28.

1 Photocopy or trace the pattern onto the firm paper with the marker pen. Use this as your master copy. This allows you to use the pattern repeatedly without damaging your book.

2 Trace three strips of the pattern, including the numbers, which indicate the sewing sequence.

3 Sort the fabrics from dark to light. Cut them out roughly and lay them in the order in which they will be sewn. This will give you the look of the quilt, even before it is sewn. Any fabrics that are in the wrong place in the sequence will 'jump out' at you.

4 Starting with piece 1, lay a coloured triangle on the back of the interfacing with the right side up and covering position 1, allowing a 6 mm (1/4 in) seam allowance. Lay piece 2 (black) over the coloured piece with the right sides together. Turn the interfacing over and stitch on the line between pieces 1 and 2, starting three stitches before the line and finishing three stitches after it. Trim the seam and flip piece 2 back. Press.

5 Continue in this manner, sewing, trimming, flipping and pressing, until the entire strip is pieced. Note that the last piece is a long strip of black fabric.

6 Cut two sashing strips, 2.2 cm (7/8 in) wide and the length of the pieced strips. Sew the sashing between the pieced strips.

TO FINISH

1 Cut two borders, 8 cm x 25 cm (3 in x 10 in) and two borders 8 cm x 35 cm (3 in x 15 in). Attach the borders to the quilt front, following the instructions for mitred borders on page 11.

2 Cut out six triangles to be appliquéd 'freehand' and pin them on in a pleasing layout. Baste the edges of the triangles under, then appliqué them in place.

3 Sew on the beads, tapering off to one corner.

4 Place the backing face down with the wadding on top and the quilt front on top of that, face upwards. Pin and baste the three layers together.

5 Quilt as desired.

6 Bind and label your quilt.

YOU WILL NEED

- **30 cm (12 in) of black fabric for the background and borders**
- **30 cm x 35 cm (12 in x 15 in) of wadding**
- **30 cm x 35 cm (12 in x 15 in) of fabric for the backing**
- **small amount of plain fabrics for the 'geese'**
- **assortment of small coloured beads**
- **medium-weight interfacing**
- **sewing machine**
- **usual sewing supplies**
- **sewing threads to blend with the fabrics**
- **rotary cutter and mat**
- **quilter's ruler**
- **firm white paper**
- **masking tape**
- **sharp pencil**
- **fineline marker pen**
- **pressing cloth**

Left: Detail of the appliqué and beading on Celebrate 111

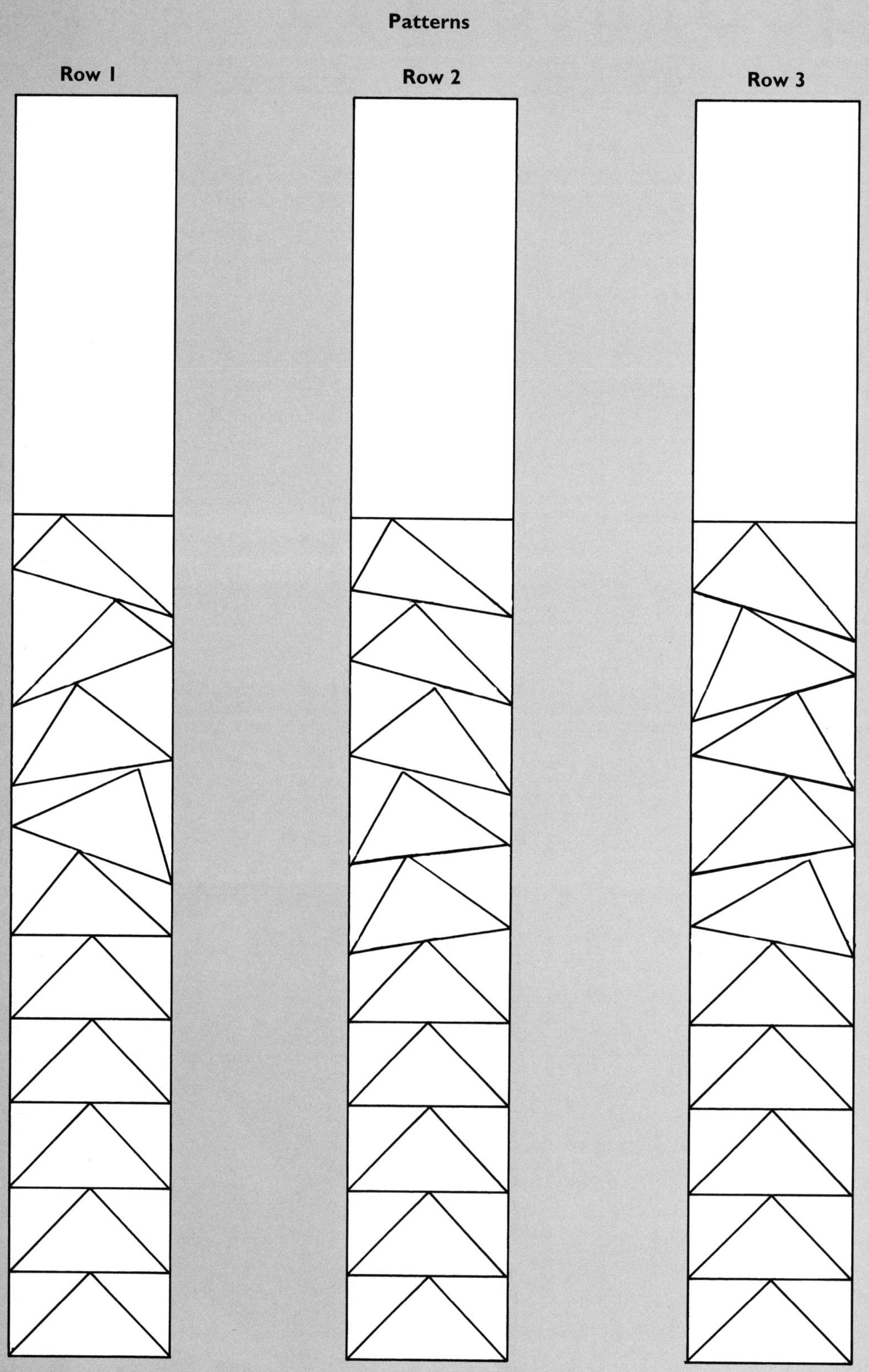

Patterns

Row 1

Row 2

Row 3

Cream
PEPPERMINT

Crazy Crayons

YOU WILL NEED

- variety of 15 cm (6 in) squares of five or six coordinating fabrics
- 15 cm x 20 cm (6 in x 8 in) of black fabric for the inner border
- 30 cm (12 in) square of bright print for the outer border
- 10 cm (4 in) of medium-weight interfacing
- 10 cm (4 in) of fabric for the binding
- 30 cm (12 in) square of wadding
- 30 cm (12 in) square of fabric for the backing
- sewing machine
- usual sewing supplies
- sewing thread to blend with the fabrics
- firm white paper
- sharp pencil
- fineline marker pen
- masking tape
- rotary cutter and mat
- quilter's ruler
- pressing cloth

The unusual fabric in the border of this quilt was a scrap from the hem of my daughter's favourite dress. When I started making miniature quilts, I knew I had to make one with this special scrap. I chose colours from the print and a simple design that I felt would work with the style of fabric. The finished piece reminded us of the crayons they played with as children – hence the name of the quilt.

The quilt can be made with all the blocks sewn on the same foundation. To add variety to the shapes in the blocks, I traced the blocks the same but, when sewing them, I changed the lines slightly by sewing outside or inside the line.

Have fun and create your own individual look with this quilt.

Machine-pieced on foundation and machine-quilted
Finished size: 26 cm ($10^1/2$ in) square
Block size: 5 cm (2 in)

INSTRUCTIONS

See the Pattern on this page.

1 Photocopy or trace the pattern onto the firm paper with the marker pen. Use this as your master copy. This allows you to use the pattern repeatedly without damaging your book.
2 Tape the tracing to a firm surface. Trace the nine blocks onto the interfacing, using the pencil. Alter some of the lines to vary your blocks, if you wish.
3 Piece the blocks following the general instructions for foundation piecing on page 9. Press the finished blocks, then trim them with the rotary cutter, leaving a 6 mm ($^1/4$ in) seam allowance on all sides of the block.
4 Experiment with the layout of the finished blocks to give a balanced look to the quilt. Join the blocks together into three rows of three blocks, then join the three rows together.

TO FINISH

1 Cut the inner border 3 cm ($1^1/4$ in) wide and the outer border 6 cm ($2^1/2$ in) wide. Sew the inner border to the quilt sides first, then to the remaining sides of the quilt. Sew the outer border in the same manner.
2 Lay the backing fabric face down with the wadding on top and the quilt front on top of that, face upwards. Pin and baste the three layers together.
3 Quilt in the ditch around the inner border.
4 Bind and label your quilt.

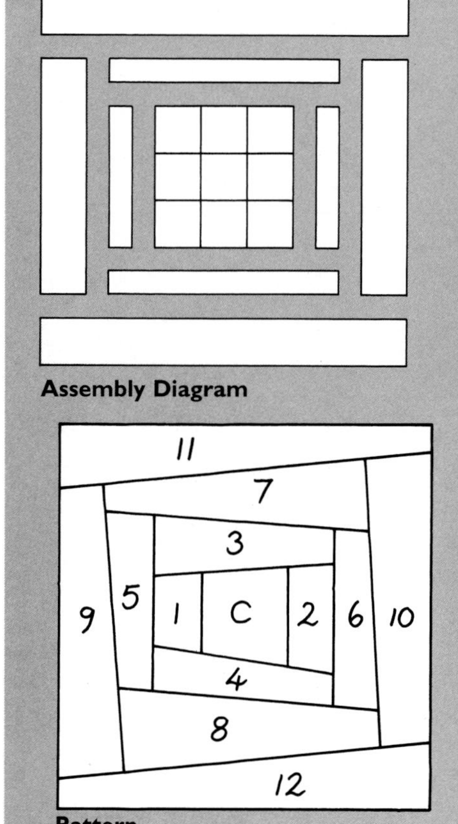

Assembly Diagram

Pattern

WASHABLE
Crayola
CRAYON
BINNEY & SMITH INC. EASTON, PA 18044-0431
MADE IN U.S.A.

Japanese Ladies

YOU WILL NEED

- four 30 cm (12 in) squares of coordinating Japanese-style fabrics
- 10 cm (4 in) of burgundy fabric for the borders and binding
- 10 cm (4 in) of fabric for the background
- 10 cm (4 in) of medium-weight interfacing
- four buttons
- sewing machine
- usual sewing supplies
- sewing threads to coordinate with the fabrics
- firm white paper
- sharp pencil
- template plastic
- masking tape
- fineline marker pen
- pressing cloth

Detail of one block

What to do with a bundle of beautiful Japanese fabrics bought at a quilt show? These fabrics are always tempting to buy, but then they sit on the shelf as I wonder how to use them. There is never enough to make a large quilt, but just enough for a tiny one.

Sifting through my mother's button box I found the buttons which were perfect for the hats, and the quilt design came together.

Machine-pieced on foundation and machine-quilted
Finished size: 24 cm x 29 cm (9 1/2 in x 11 1/2 in)
Block size: 5 cm x 6.5 cm (2 in x 2 1/2 in)

INSTRUCTIONS

See the Pattern and the Templates on page 34.
Note: The ladies are pieced on foundation, while templates are given for the other pieces. Remember to add seam allowances when you cut out the fabric pieces using the templates.

For the blocks

1. Photocopy or trace the pattern onto the firm paper with the marker pen. Use this as your master copy. This allows you to use the pattern repeatedly without damaging your book.
2. Tape the tracing to a firm surface and trace four patterns onto the interfacing, using the pencil. Include the numbers, as they indicate the sequence of sewing.
3. Piece the four blocks, following the general instructions for foundation piecing on page 9. Press the finished blocks, then trim the edges with the rotary cutter, allowing 6 mm (1/4 in) seam allowances on all sides.

For the quilt centre

1. Trace templates A, B and C onto the template plastic and cut them out. Remember, the templates are finished size, so you will need to add 6 mm (1/4 in) seam allowances when you cut them from the fabric.
2. Place the templates on the back of the background fabric and draw round them with the pencil. Cut out two A, two B and four C. Cut one piece from the background fabric the same size as the foundation blocks.
3. Lay out the background pieces with the completed foundation blocks. Join them into rows, then join the rows together.

TO FINISH

1. Cut the borders 2.5 cm (1 in) wide. Sew them to two opposite sides of the centre, then to the two other sides.
2. The outer triangles can be cut from one piece of fabric, using template D or you can piece squares together, then cut out the triangles. Use E for the squares. Join the outer triangles to the quilt.
3. Lay the backing fabric face down with the wadding on top and the quilt front on top of that, face upwards. Press the three layers together gently. Pin and baste the three layers together.
4. Machine-quilt in the ditch around the inner border.
5. Bind and label your quilt.

Liberty Baskets

Liberty fabrics are wonderful for miniature quilts. The range of colours and the variety of tiny prints enhance your finished work. Four tiny baskets were featured on a USA stamp, hence the name of the block, Postage Stamp Baskets.

Machine-pieced on foundation, hand-quilted
Finished size: 38 cm (15 in) square
Block size: 7.5 cm (3 in)

INSTRUCTIONS

See the Pattern on page 36.

1 Photocopy or trace the pattern onto the firm paper with the marker pen. Use this as your master copy. This allows you to use the pattern repeatedly without damaging your book.

2 Tape the patterns onto a firm surface and trace the patterns onto the interfacing, using the pencil. Make nine copies of A, and eighteen copies each of B and C.

3 Refer to the general instructions for foundation piecing on page 9. Starting with section A, cut a cream square roughly to the size required plus 6 mm (1/4 in) seam allowances. Place it in the centre of the interfacing. Lay a print triangle over the cream fabric with the right sides together. Pin to hold. Turn the interfacing over and sew on the line between the square and the triangle. Flip the fabric over and press. Add the remaining three triangles to the interfacing, press, then trim leaving a 6 mm (1/4 in) seam allowance on each side.

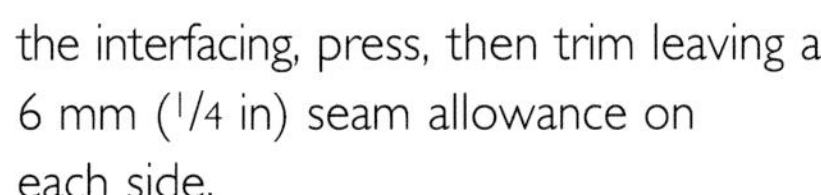

4 Make the remaining segments B and C of the block in the same manner. Be careful to match up the fabric for the basket base to the basket triangle in the centre square (Fig. 1). Press and trim them, leaving a 6 mm (1/4 in) seam allowance on each side. Make one complete block first to check that the fabrics match.

5 Lay out all the segments of the block. Add the shorter sides first with a large stitch. Check that all the points meet, then oversew with a small stitch. Add the other two segments.

6 Complete the remaining blocks in the same manner.

7 Make a template of the handle from cardboard or template plastic. Using the pencil, lightly mark the template onto each block. Stem stitch the handles in a coloured thread to coordinate with the basket fabric.

Left: Detail of the block

YOU WILL NEED

- 40 cm (16 in) of cream fabric for the background, borders and binding
- variety of coordinating scraps for the baskets
- stranded embroidery cotton for embroidering the handles
- 10 cm (4 in) of medium-weight interfacing
- 45 cm (18 in) square of wadding
- 45 cm (18 in) square of fabric for the backing
- 15 cm (6 in) square of clear Contact paper
- sewing machine
- usual sewing supplies
- sewing threads to blend with the fabrics
- cream quilting thread
- firm white paper
- sharp pencil
- fineline marker pen
- masking tape
- pressing cloth

TO FINISH

1 Lay the completed blocks out and decide on a pleasing layout. Sew the blocks into three rows of three blocks. Sew with a large stitch first, check that all the points match up, then oversew with a smaller stitch.

2 Cut four borders from the cream fabric, 9 cm x 43 cm (3½ in x 17 in). Add the borders, following the general instructions for mitred borders on page 11.

3 Lay the backing fabric face down with the wadding on top and the quilt front on top of that, face upwards. Pin and baste the three layers together.

4 Trace the basket pattern onto Contact paper as many times as required for the quilting pattern. Each Contact paper pattern can be used a few times. Cut them out and stick them in the border in a pleasing layout. Quilt around the basket outlines, remove the Contact paper and quilt the centre lines. Quilt through the centres of the blocks.

5 Bind and label your quilt.

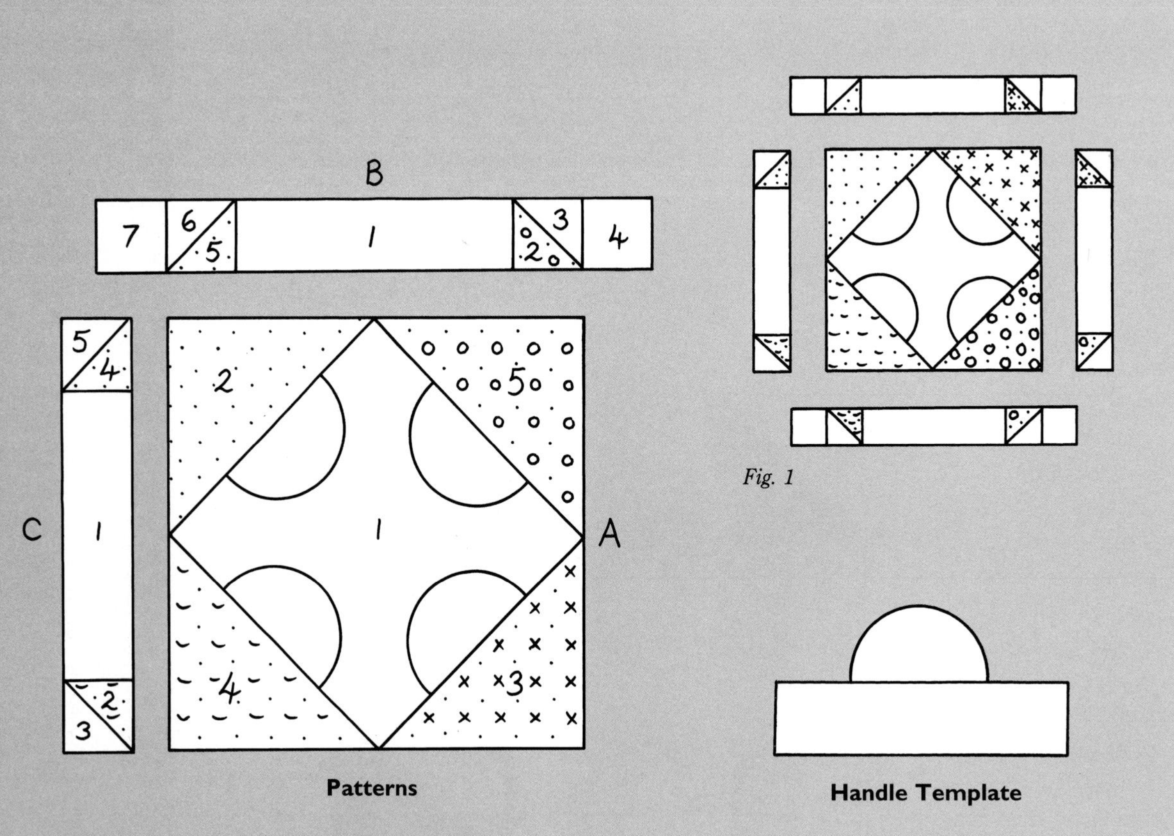

Patterns

Fig. 1

Handle Template

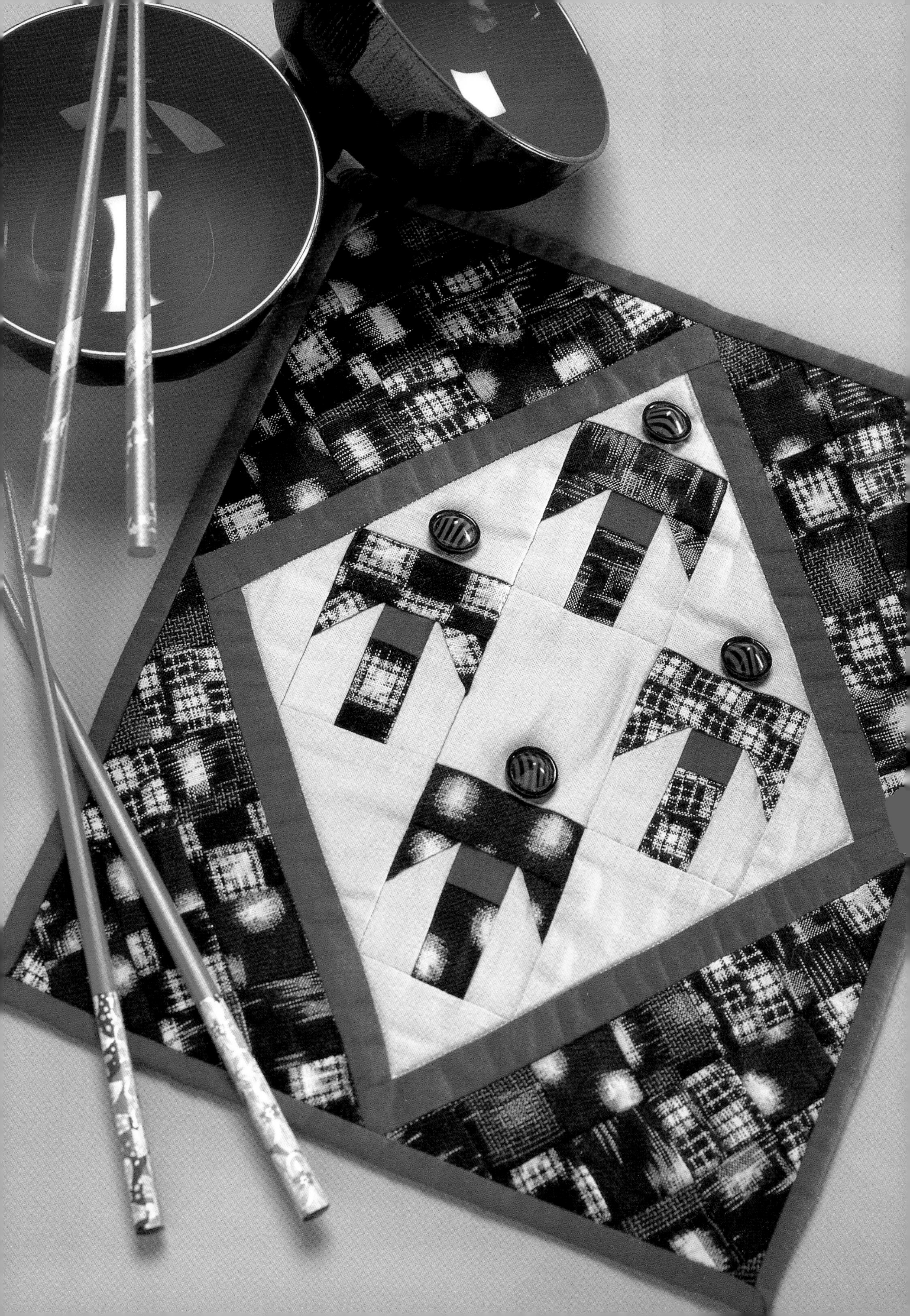

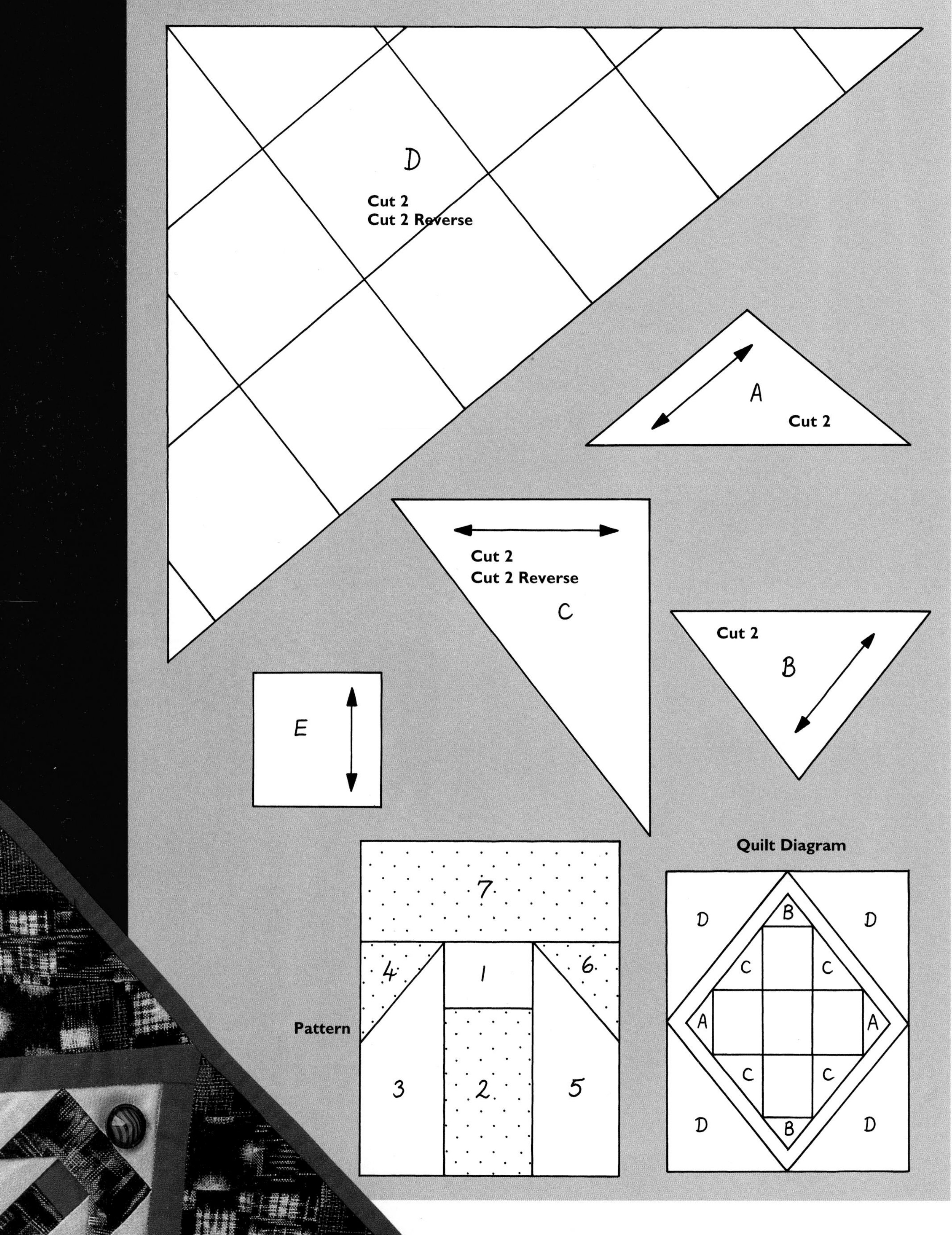
D
Cut 2
Cut 2 Reverse
A
Cut 2
Cut 2
Cut 2 Reverse
C
Cut 2
B
E
Quilt Diagram
7
4
1
6
Pattern
3
2
5
D
D
B
C
C
A
A
C
C
D
B
D

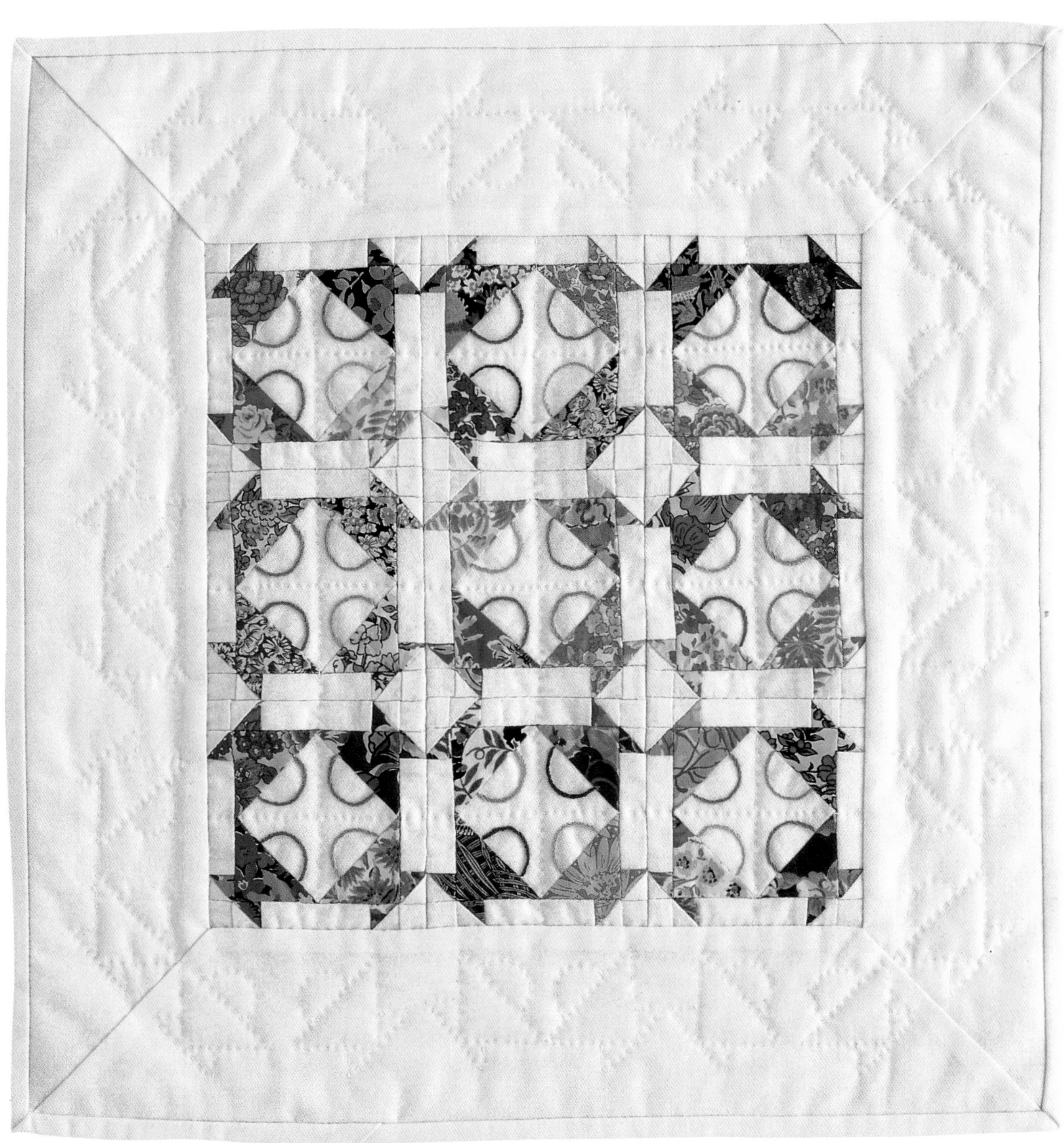

Shaded Four-patch

YOU WILL NEED

- **7.5 cm (3 in) squares of sixteen dark fabrics**
- **7.5 cm (3 in) squares of twenty lighter fabrics**
- **20 cm (8 in) of fabric for the background**
- **15 cm x 30 cm (6 in x 12 in) each of fabric for the inner border, outer border and bindings**
- **20 cm (8 in) of medium-weight interfacing**
- **sewing machine**
- **usual sewing supplies**
- **sewing threads to blend with the fabrics**
- **firm white paper**
- **sharp pencil**
- **fineline marker pen**
- **masking tape**
- **pressing cloth**

Detail of four blocks

Blue quilts have a special attraction for me. Blue is the colour of calm and tranquillity – hence our blue bedroom with blue quilts. My scrap bag has a vast array of blue scraps.

Traditional or contemporary? This will depend on the style of fabric you choose. Scraps that are all of a similar intensity (all light or all dark) will give a more traditional look. Sometimes, no matter how hard you try to control the look of a scrap quilt, the final result can be unpredictable.

An even number of light and dark fabrics enabled me to play with the finished blocks and decide on the dark centre and corners. The centre row is composed of both light and medium fabrics. This quilt is made with sixteen dark and twenty lighter fabrics.

If you feel that the block is too small for you to work with comfortably, enlarge the pattern on the photocopier to the size that suits you best.

Machine-pieced on foundation and machine-quilted
Finished size: 35 cm (14 in) square
Block size: 3.5 cm (1 1/2 in)

INSTRUCTIONS

See the Pattern on page 40.

1. Photocopy or trace the pattern onto the firm paper with the marker pen. Use this as your master copy. This allows you to use the pattern repeatedly without damaging your book.
2. Tape the pattern onto a firm surface and trace thirty-six blocks onto the interfacing, using the pencil. As the sewing sequence is simple, add the number to a few blocks to start with, but you'll find it's not necessary for all the blocks.
3. Piece the blocks, following the general instructions for foundation piecing on page 9. Press the finished blocks, then trim the edges, allowing 6 mm (1/4 in) seam allowances on all sides of the block.
4. Lay out the blocks in six rows of six blocks (Fig. 1). This may take a while; as you play with the blocks you will find many different possibilities. Before sewing them together look at your quilt through the viewfinder of a camera or a front door peephole. You will be surprised how clear the pattern becomes and any 'mistakes' will jump out at you.
5. Sew the blocks together into rows, then sew the rows together. Remember to use a large stitch first, check that all the little points are accurate, then overstitch with a smaller stitch. Take your time doing this and be prepared to fiddle with them. It's better to take the time and make sure that the points are as accurate as possible, rather than forever being annoyed by a mistake – which is always in the centre of the quilt.
6. Cut the inner border 2.5 cm x 38 cm (1 in x 15 in) and the outer border 6 cm x 38 cm (2.5 in x 15 in). Sew the borders together and press the seam towards the wider border. Attach the borders to the quilt, following the instructions for mitred corners on page 11.
7. Lay the backing face down with the wadding on top and the quilt front on top of that, face upwards. Pin and baste the three layers together.
8. Quilt in the ditch around the inner border.
9. Bind and label your quilt.

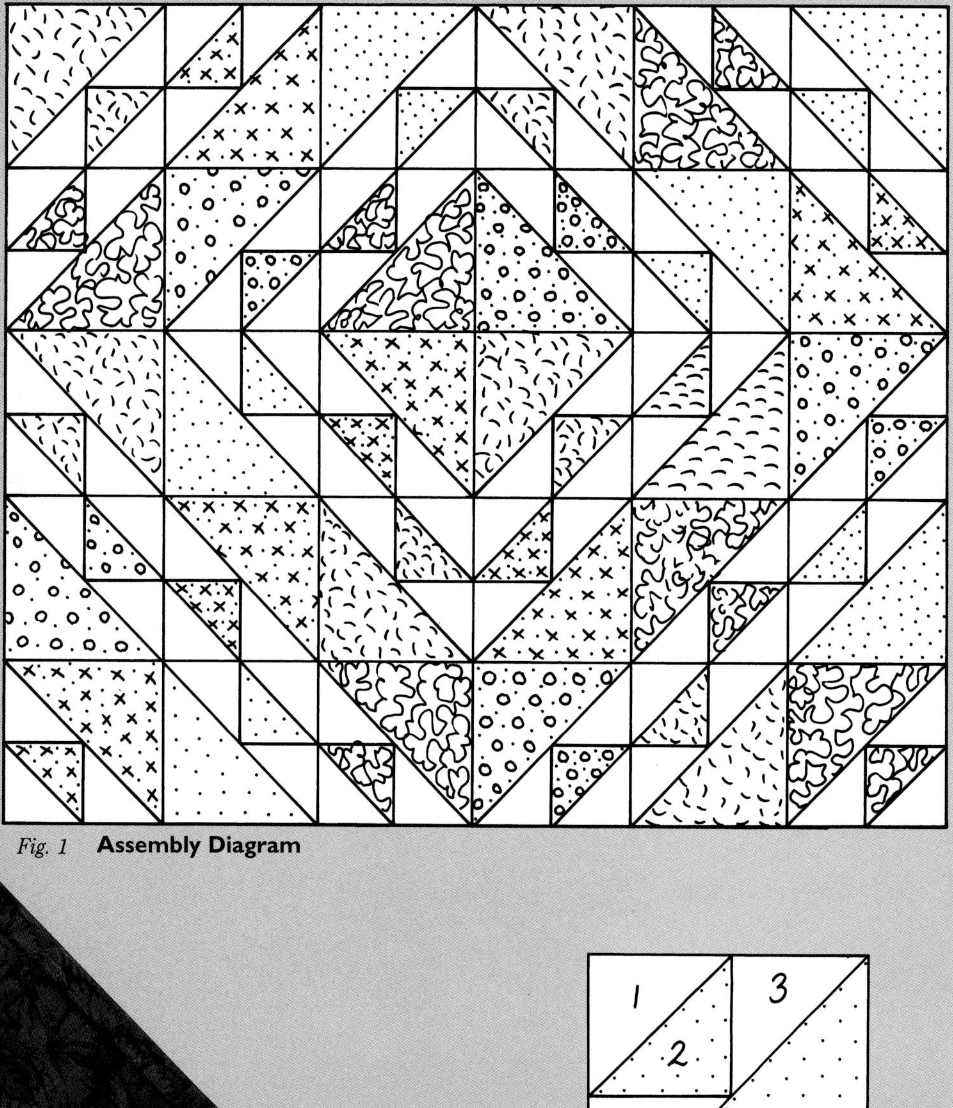

Fig. 1 **Assembly Diagram**

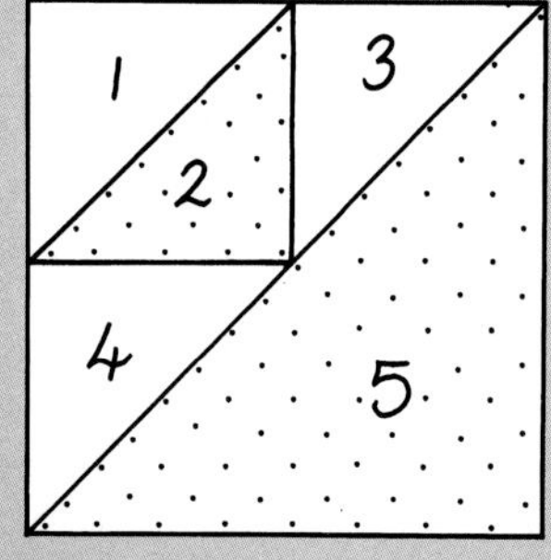

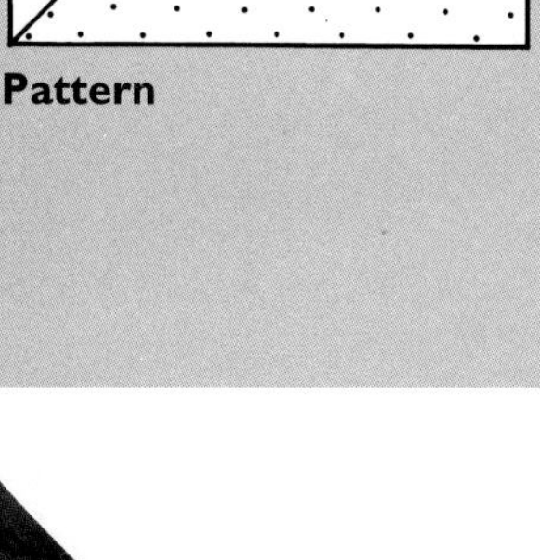

Pattern

Baby Mist

Treasured scraps collected from your favourite quilts or scraps from a quilt you may have given away come together to create a tiny masterpiece.

Sample swatches of fabric from a patchwork shop were the beginning of this quilt. Often they are too small and fiddly to actually cut and sew together, but this pattern, worked on a foundation, is an ideal way to use them. I sorted the fabrics into lights and darks which gave a sharp contrast within the quilt. When I took out the darkest fabrics, the remaining fabrics were in the medium range, giving a lovely soft contrast with the light fabrics.

Scraps of similar intensity of colour and with small floral patterns give this quilt a soft feel. The pattern is simple and can be worked on the machine or by hand quite easily. Draw up your foundation, grab your scraps, keep them in a little bag and you'll have an easy piece to work on in those spare moments.

Machine-pieced on foundation and hand-quilted
Finished size: 23 cm x 28 cm (9 in x 11 in)

INSTRUCTIONS

See the Patterns on page 42.

1 Photocopy or trace the pattern onto the firm paper with the marker pen. Use this as your master copy. This allows you to use the pattern repeatedly without damaging your book.

2 Tape the pattern onto a firm surface, then tape the interfacing over the top and trace the pattern onto the interfacing, using the pencil. Remember that your finished block will only be as accurate as your tracing, so use a sharp pencil and trace accurately.

3 Trace seven copies of pattern 1, two copies of pattern 2 and two copies of pattern 3. The finished work will be the reverse of the tracing. Roughly shade the interfacing, indicating the medium and light sequence.

4 Sort your fabrics into two piles – light and medium. Play with them till you have a pleasing assortment. Cut the fabric roughly the size of the finished triangles, allowing 6 mm (1/4 in) seam allowances and a bit more.

5 Set the stitch length on your machine to 5-6 stitches per centimetre (12-15 per inch) or approximately 1.5-2 stitch length and work with an open-toed or appliqué foot on your machine.

6 Start with pattern 1 and lay a medium fabric in position on the back of the interfacing (right side up), allowing a 6 mm (1/4 in) seam allowance. Hold the interfacing up to the light and check that the piece is in the right position. Lay the next fabric (light) over it with the right

Detail of the block

YOU WILL NEED

- 30 cm (12 in) of cream homespun for the inner border and binding
- variety of scraps in the light and medium ranges
- 20 cm (8 in) of medium-weight interfacing
- 30 cm x 35 cm (12 in x 14 in) of wadding
- 30 cm x 35 cm (12 in x 14 in) of fabric for the backing
- sewing machine
- usual sewing supplies
- rotary cutter and mat
- quilter's ruler
- sewing threads to blend with the fabrics
- cream quilting thread
- firm white paper
- fineline marker pen
- sharp pencil
- masking tape
- pressing cloth

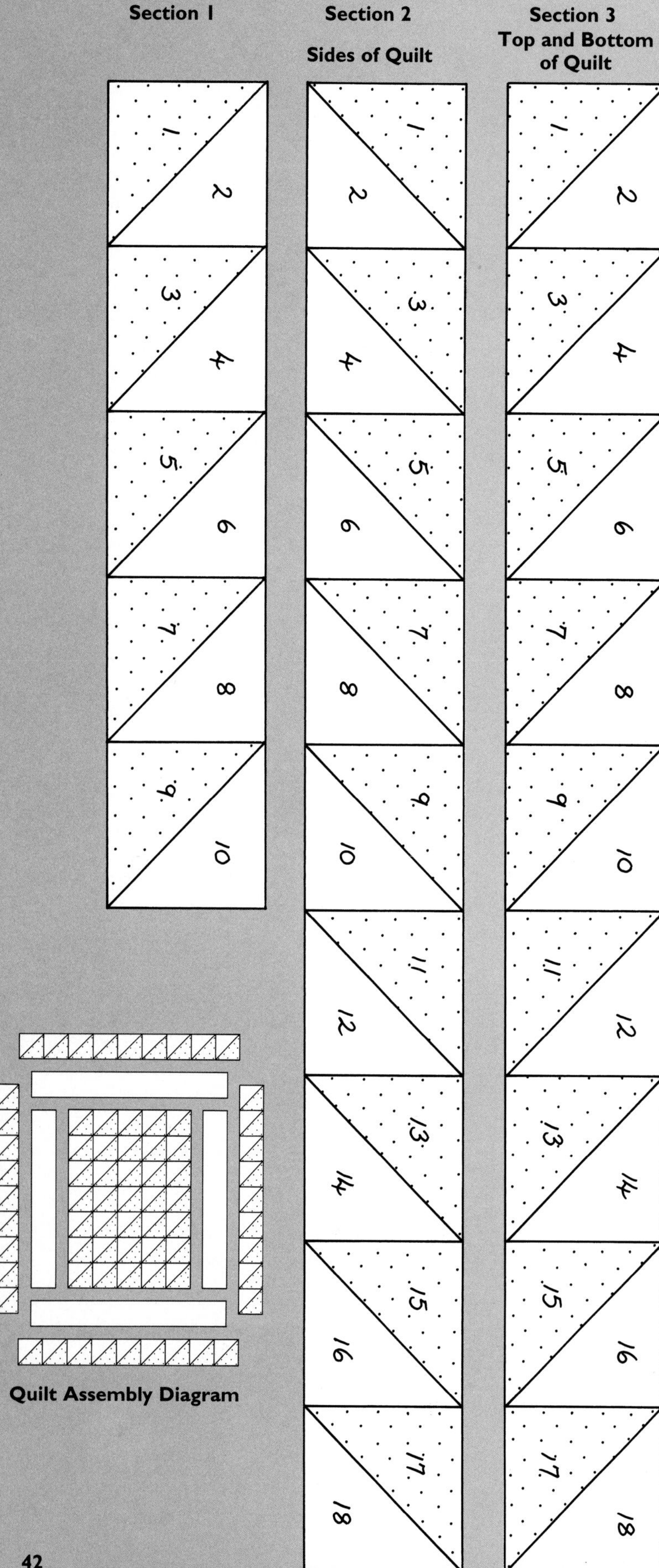

Quilt Assembly Diagram

sides together. Sew along the drawn line between pieces 1 and 2, starting three stitches before the line and finishing three stitches after it. This allows for the seam allowances. Carefully trim the seam, if necessary, and flip the second fabric over. Press, then lay the third fabric down and sew, trim, flip and press, as before. Continue working in this manner, alternating the light and medium fabrics till the row is finished.

7 Press the strip, then trim the edges, allowing 6 mm (1/4 in) seam allowances on all sides of the strip.

8 Complete seven strips, then decide in which order you want to sew them together. Sew the rows together with a large stitch, check that the points of the triangles meet, then oversew the seam with a smaller stitch.

TO FINISH

1 Cut two strips of cream fabric, each 3.7 cm (1 1/2 in) and the length of the quilt. Sew them to the sides of the centre piece. Press the seams. Cut two strips of cream fabric, each 3.7 cm (1 1/2 in) and the width of the quilt. Sew them to the top and bottom of the centre piece.

2 Sew the remaining border foundations in the same manner as for the centre piece, following the medium and light sequence. Press the finished strips and trim, allowing 6 mm (1/4 in) seam allowances on all sides. Sew the side strips on first, then the top and bottom strips. Press the quilt top using the iron to block your work.

3 Lay the backing fabric face down with the wadding on top and the quilt front on top of that, face upwards. Pin and baste the three layers together.

4 Hand-quilt a diagonal grid right across the quilt.

5 Bind and label your quilt.

Cabins in the Country

YOU WILL NEED

- 30 cm (12 in) of fabric for the background
- nine fat quarters of fabric: three each of red, blue and green
- fat quarter for the stars
- fat quarter for the roofs
- 10 cm (4 in) of fabric for the inner border
- 20 cm (8 in) of fabric for the outer border
- 10 cm (4 in) of fabric for the binding
- 60 cm (24 in) square of fabric for the backing
- 60 cm (24 in) square of wadding
- scrap of cream homespun
- pearl buttons
- 20 cm (8 in) of medium-weight interfacing
- sewing machine
- rotary cutter and mat
- quilter's ruler
- pencil
- usual sewing supplies
- sewing thread to blend with the fabrics
- pressing cloth
- firm white paper
- fineline marker pen
- masking tape

In this quilt, country fabrics create the appropriate look in the nine little blocks. A collection of red, green and blue fat quarters are required plus fabric for the stars and roofs. As a finishing touch, trim the trees with your favourite buttons.

Machine-pieced on foundation and machine-quilted
Finished size: 50 cm (19½ in) square
Block size: 11 cm (4¼ in)

INSTRUCTIONS

See the Patterns on page 46.
Photocopy or trace the patterns onto the firm paper with the marker pen. Use this as your master copy. This allows you to use the pattern repeatedly without damaging your book. You can then tape the patterns onto a firm surface and trace them onto the interfacing using the pencil.

For the Tree block

1 Trace the patterns onto the interfacing. Include the numbers, as they indicate the order of sewing. Leave enough room around each block tracing for the 6 mm (¼ in) seam allowance.

2 Referring to the general instructions for foundation piecing on page 9, piece the three Tree blocks. Press the finished blocks and trim, leaving a 6 mm (¼ in) seam allowance on all sides of the block.

3 To add the log cabin strips, cut three different red strips, each 2.5 cm x 25 cm (1 in x 10 in). Sew one strip to the side of one Tree block. Trim and press. Sew the same strip across the bottom of the block. Trim and press. Add the remaining red strips in the same manner. Cut the blue and green fabric strips and add them to the remaining blocks in the same way (Fig. 1).

4 Sew on the buttons. Fray a narrow strip of homespun, tie a knot in the centre and attach it to the top of the tree.

For the House and Star blocks

The House and Star blocks are sewn in the same manner as the Tree block.

Detail of the Tree block

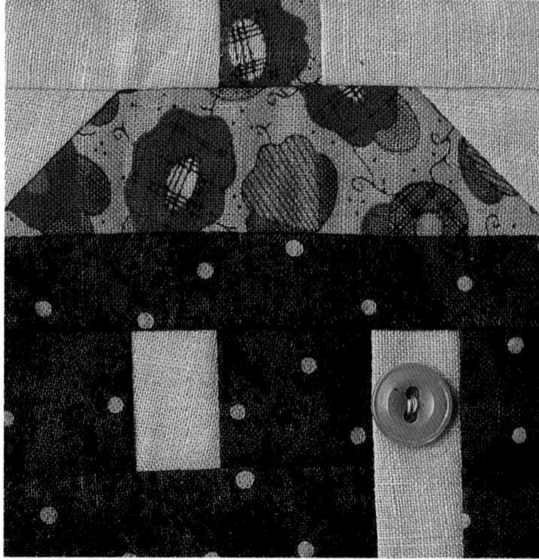
Detail of the House block

Detail of the Star block

TO FINISH

1 Using the photograph as a guide, lay out the blocks in three rows of three, then sew them together (Fig. 2).

2 Cut the inner border 2.5 cm x 52 cm (1 in x 21 in) and the outer border 7 cm x 52 cm (3 in x 21 in). Sew the inner border to the outer border and press the seam to the outer border. Add the borders following the general instructions for mitred borders on page 11.

3 Lay the backing fabric face down with the wadding on top and the quilt front on top of that, face upwards. Pin and baste the three layers together.

4 Quilt in the ditch around the star, house and tree squares and the borders.

5 Bind and label your quilt.

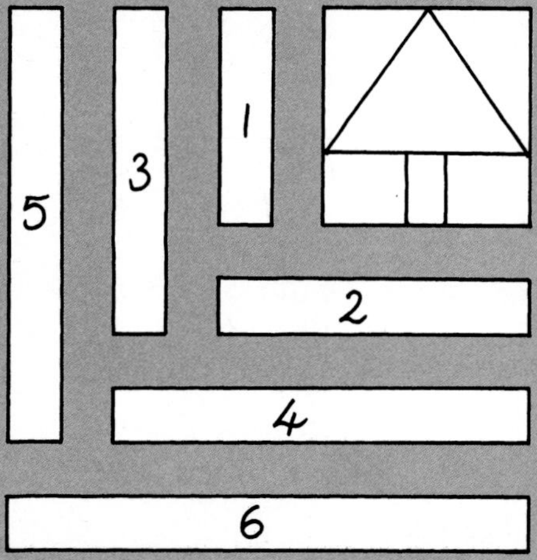

5 3 1 2 4 6

Fig. 1

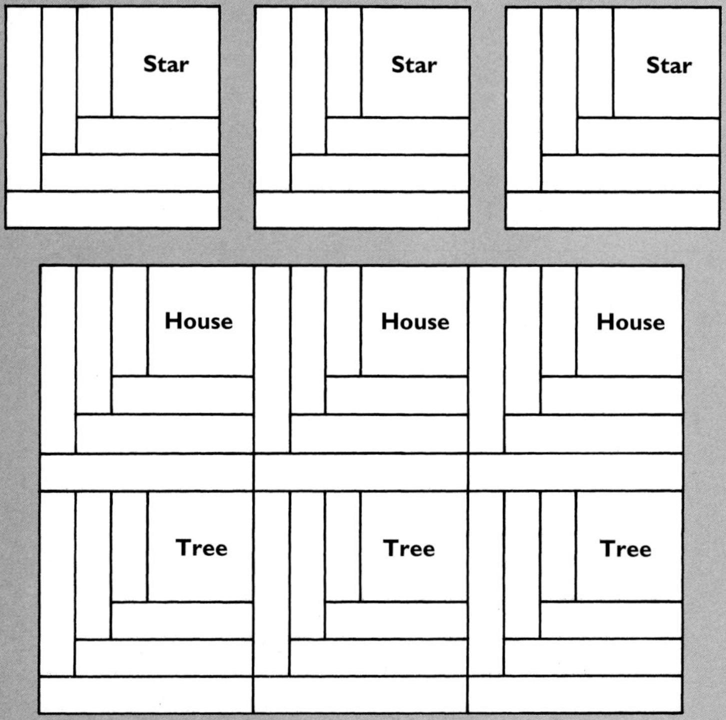

Star Star Star
House House House
Tree Tree Tree

Fig. 2

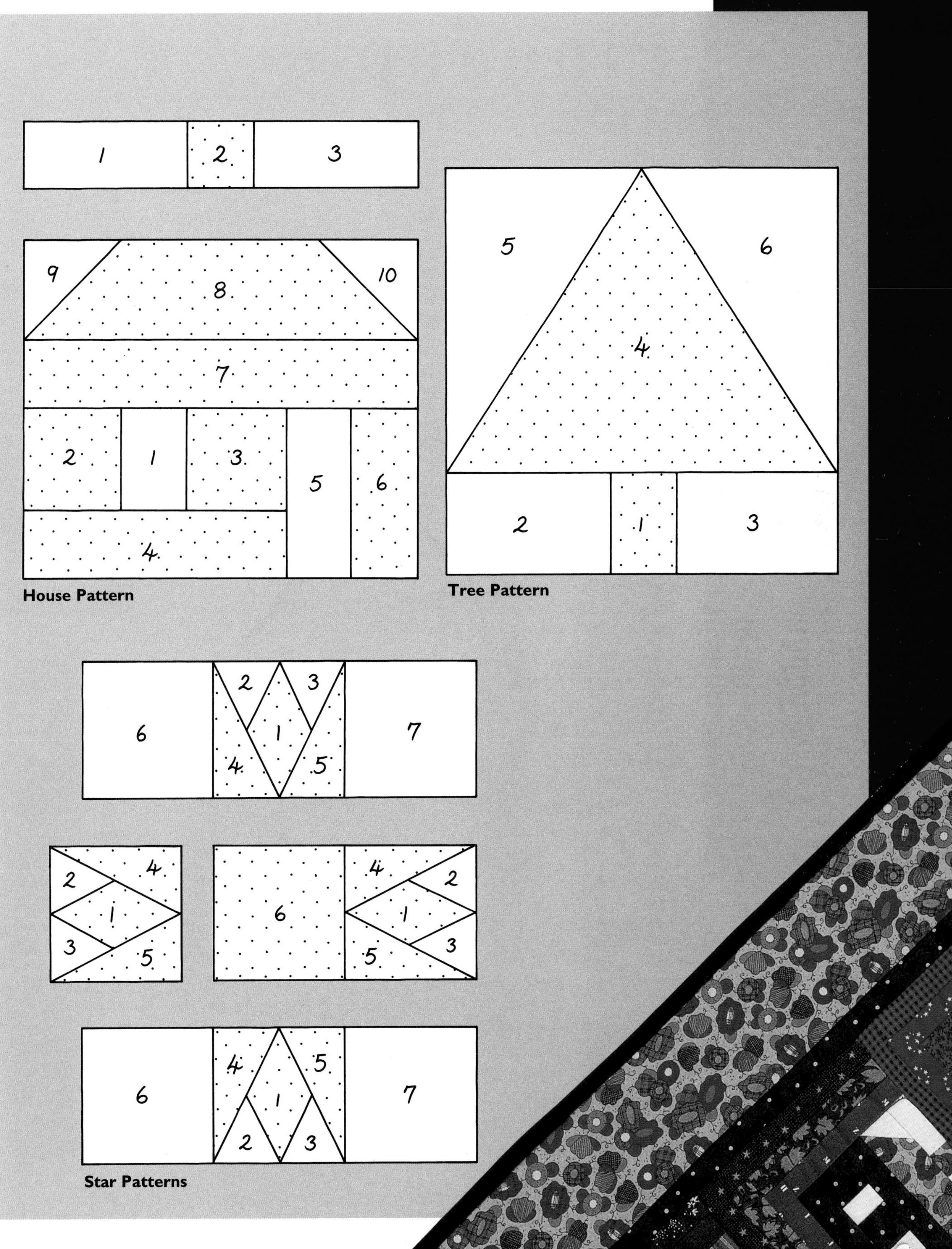

House Pattern

Tree Pattern

Star Patterns

Pineapple

YOU WILL NEED

- a fat quarter each of red and green fabric
- a variety of beige scraps
- 10 cm (4 in) of green polished cotton for the wide border
- 10 cm (4 in) of burgundy fabric for the narrow border and binding
- 10 cm (4 in) of medium-weight interfacing
- 20 cm (8 in) square of wadding
- 20 cm (8 in) square of fabric for the backing
- sewing machine
- usual sewing supplies
- sewing threads to blend with the fabrics
- sharp pencil
- firm white paper
- fineline marker pen
- masking tape
- pressing cloth

pattern

Some of you may be wondering why two blocks in this quilt have different-coloured centres. I entered this quilt in a miniature quilt challenge which required you to make a miniature quilt using the teal and gold fabric provided. Teal and gold doesn't fit my colour scheme at home hence the tiny amount used. My quilt looked out of place next to all the others, but I did win the challenge!

When working on such a tiny foundation it is necessary to use an open-toed or appliqué foot on your machine to see exactly where you are sewing. Plain fabrics, tone-on-tone fabric or tiny prints are the best choice for this project.

Machine-pieced on foundation
Finished size: approximately 17 cm (6½ in) square
Block size: 3.8 cm (1½ in)

INSTRUCTIONS

See the Pattern on this page.

1 Photocopy or trace the pattern onto the firm paper with the marker pen. Use this as your master copy. This allows you to use the pattern repeatedly without damaging your book.

2 Tape the pattern onto a firm surface and trace nine blocks onto the interfacing, using the pencil. As the pattern is so tiny use a sharp pencil and be very accurate. You may like to use coloured pencils and shade the red and green sections.
In the beginning, when you're flipping and sewing, this helps to keep the design clear.

3 Starting in the centre of the block, lay the green centre piece 1 down, right side out. Lay piece 2 over the centre square, right sides together, and sew the seam between pieces 1 and 2. You will need to have a tiny stitch length set on your machine. This can be a problem if you make a mistake, so be prepared to throw out a block if you have trouble undoing the tiny stitches.

4 Sew the first four triangles in the same manner. Press the block, then add the next round of triangles and press. Continue in this manner, following the numbering sequence until all the pieces have been added.

Note: The finished strips in the block are very fine. Using normal sewing principles, you would trim the seams shorter than the next stitching line. As the strips are so tiny, I leave them longer so they sit under the next row of stitching. If they were cut too fine they could fray.

5 Complete all the blocks. Press and trim, leaving a 6 mm (¼ in) seam allowance round each block.

6 Lay out the blocks in three rows of three blocks. Join them into rows, then join the rows. Join the blocks with a large stitch first, check that everything lines up, then oversew with a smaller stitch.

TO FINISH

1 Cut the burgundy inner border 1.5 cm (⅝ in) wide and the outer border 3.8 cm (1½ in) wide.

2 Sew the inner border to the quilt, then add the outer border.

3 Lay the backing fabric face down with the wadding on top and the quilt front on top of that, face upwards. Press the three layers together gently. As this quilt is so tiny, I decided not to quilt it.

4 Bind and label your quilt.

Amish Schoolhouses

YOU WILL NEED

- **40 cm (16 in) of black homespun for the background, borders and binding**
- **15 cm (6 in) squares of nine plain fabrics for the houses**
- **35 cm (14 in) of fabric for the backing**
- **35 cm (14 in) of wadding**
- **20 cm (8 in) of medium-weight interfacing**
- **sewing machine**
- **rotary cutter and mat (optional)**
- **quilter's ruler (optional)**
- **usual sewing supplies**
- **sewing thread to blend with the fabrics**
- **pressing cloth**
- **sharp pencil**
- **firm white paper**
- **fineline marker pen**
- **masking tape**

Amish quilts are easily recognised by their use of mainly black and plain-coloured fabrics, the simplicity of the design and the inner glow that emerges from the combination of these. Made from their clothing scraps the quilts reflect the plain and simple lifestyle of the Amish.

Machine-pieced on foundation and hand-quilted
Finished size: 29 cm (11 1/2 in) square
Block size: 5 cm (2 in)

INSTRUCTIONS

See the Pattern on page 52.
Note: The Schoolhouse block is more complex than other foundation work, but if you follow the directions, the results will be very satisfying. Three foundation sections are needed to complete the block. Each section is sewn, then trimmed, allowing a 6 mm (1/4 in) seam allowance on all sides, then the three sections are pieced together.

1. Photocopy or trace the pattern onto the firm paper with the marker pen. Use this as your master copy. This allows you to use the pattern repeatedly without damaging your book.
2. Tape the pattern onto a firm surface, then trace the Schoolhouse block onto the interfacing with the pencil, allowing 2.5 cm (1 in) between the sections. The image will be reversed when it is sewn. Be accurate and include the numbers which indicate the sequence of sewing. Shade the coloured sections.
3. Roughly cut the fabric to the size of the finished pieces, allowing 6 mm (1/4 in) seam allowances. Set the stitch length on your machine to 5-6 stitches per centimetre (12-15 stitches per inch) or approximately 1.5 stitch length and work with an open-toed or appliqué foot.
4. Start with section 1. Place piece 1 (coloured) in position on the back of the interfacing with the right side up, allowing a 6 mm (1/4 in) seam allowance. Hold the interfacing up to the light to check that the piece is in the right position.
5. Lay the piece 2 (black) in place. Pin the fabric to hold it. Turn the interfacing over and sew along the drawn line between pieces 1 and 2, starting three stitches before the line and finishing three stitches after it. This allows for the seam allowance. Carefully trim the seam allowance and flip piece 2 over. Press.
6. Lay the third fabric down and sew, trim, flip and press, as before. Keep working in this manner till piece 9 is in place.
7. Piece 10 is made of two fabrics which need to be joined before being sewn to the foundation. Sew a black and a coloured fabric together, check that the seam line matches the line on the foundation, then proceed as previously.
8. Press the finished section of the block and trim, allowing a 6 mm (1/4 in) seam allowance on all sides of the section.
9. Sew section 2 in the same manner as section 1. I find it easier if I lay the roof section down first, then add the other fabrics. Trim around the finished section, allowing a 6 mm (1/4 in) seam allowance.
10. Sew section 3 in the same way. Trim around the finished section, allowing a 6 mm (1/4 in) seam allowance.
11. Lay out the three sections, then sew them together. Sew with a large stitch

Detail of a house

first, check that the points match, then oversew with a smaller stitch.

12 Complete all nine blocks in the same manner. Lay out the completed blocks.

TO FINISH

1 Cut 2.5 cm (1 in) wide black strips for the sashing. Sew the houses into three rows with the sashing in between (Fig. 1).

2 Sew the rows together with sashing strips in between.

3 Cut the border 7 cm (3 in) wide. Add the borders, following the instructions on page 11, mitring the corners.

4 Lay the backing face down, with the wadding and the quilt front on top, face upwards. Pin and baste the three layers together. Hand- or machine-quilt in the border.

5 Bind and label your quilt.

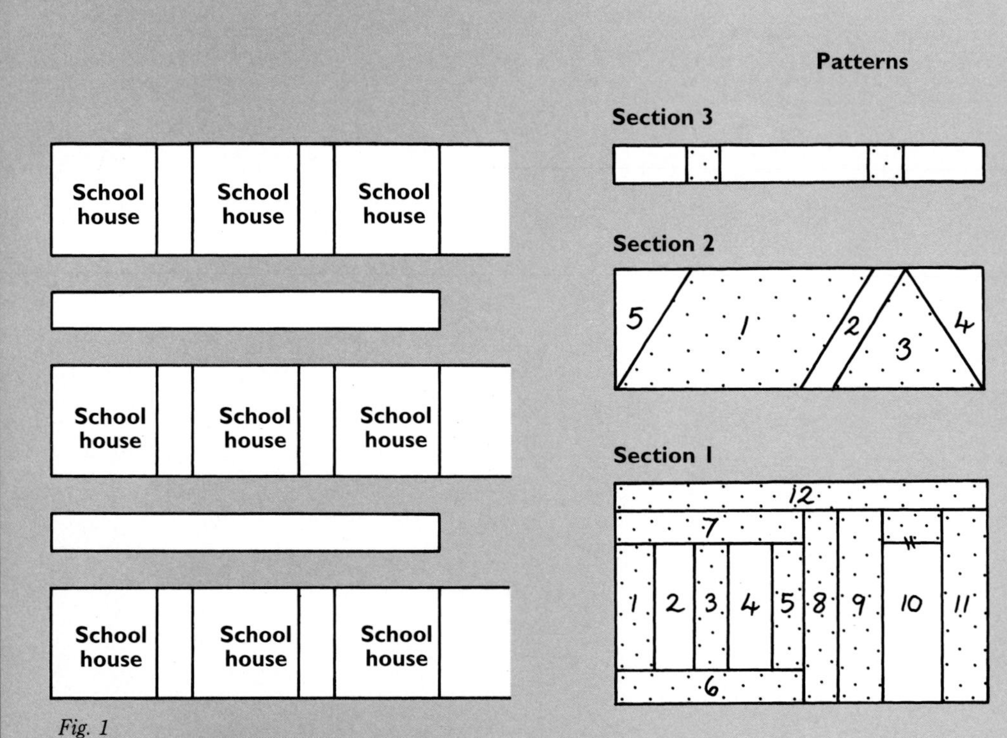

Fig. 1

Heirloom Treasure

A collection of old family lace started me on this quilt. Cream fabrics, moirés, satins and silks complement the lace. Complete the effect with beads, ribbons and charms from your collection. As a child I loved to rummage in my grandmother's sewing basket and play with all the bits and pieces that I'd find there. My girls find the same fascination with the special tin for my crazy patchwork 'bits'. You never know what you'll find.

Miniature crazy patchwork is quick and satisfying as you may only need four or five embroidery stitches and you're at the end of the row.

Machine-pieced on foundation and hand-quilted
Finished size: 27 cm (10½ in) square
Block size: 4 cm (1½ in) square

INSTRUCTIONS

See the Pattern and the Template on page 54.

1. Trace the square pattern onto the interfacing.
2. Cut a scrap of cream fabric, lay it on the centre of the interfacing. Place another piece of a different cream fabric on top, with the right sides together. Sew the seam joining them, leaving a small seam allowance. Flip the second piece over and press, using a pressing cloth (Fig. 1).
3. Continue in this way until the square is covered. I try to include four to six fabrics in each block. You may also like to include a strip of lace. Trim the block, leaving a 6 mm (¼ in) seam allowance on all sides.
4. Make nine blocks in the same way.
5. Join the blocks into three rows of three blocks as shown on page 54.

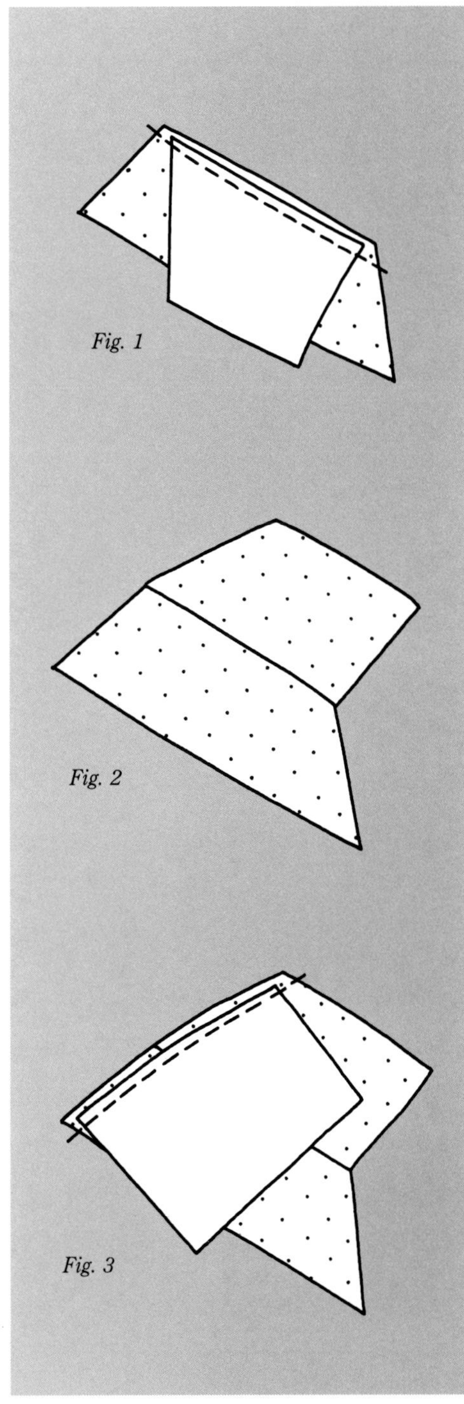

Fig. 1

Fig. 2

Fig. 3

YOU WILL NEED

- small amounts of coordinating cream silk, moiré and satin fabrics
- silk ribbons
- gold thread
- stranded cotton
- pearl buttons, beads and charms
- 50 cm (20 in) of cream homespun for the quilt top, backing and binding
- 30 cm (12 in) square of wadding
- 10 cm (4 in) of medium-weight interfacing
- quilting thread
- sewing machine
- usual sewing supplies
- sewing thread
- template plastic or cardboard
- fineline marker pen
- sharp pencil
- pressing cloth

Detail of the centre of the quilt

Pattern

Quilting Pattern

A

Template

For the embellishments

A few simple stitches and a variety of threads can create a richly textured piece of work. Feather stitch, Cretan stitch, straight stitch and buttonhole stitch have all been used in this quilt. Work all the stitches with one strand of gold thread or stranded cotton. Sew on the beads, buttons and charms.

TO FINISH

1. Trace template A onto plastic or cardboard. Remember the template is the finished size; you will need to add seam allowances. Cut out four cream triangles and sew them to the sides of the crazy patchwork section.
2. Measure the width of the quilt. Cut two 7.5 cm (3 in) wide strips the width of the quilt. Sew to two opposite sides.
3. Measure the length of the quilt. Cut two 7.5 cm (3 in) wide strips the length of the quilt. Sew them to the remaining sides.
4. Feather stitch round the crazy patchwork section, then round the border seam, using the gold thread.
5. Mark out the grid design on the borders and the little heart in the four large triangles. Layer the backing fabric, wadding and quilt top. Finely quilt with cream thread. If you are having trouble quilting tiny stitches, you may like to machine-quilt the design or even leave the piece unquilted.
6. Bind the finished piece with cream homespun unless it is to be framed.

Warm Hearts

YOU WILL NEED

- 40 cm (16 in) of fine black wool for the background
- scraps of fine wool
- 40 cm (16 in) square of wadding
- stranded embroidery cotton, Gold
- 10 cm (4 in) of homespun or interfacing
- sewing machine
- sewing thread to blend with the fabrics
- usual sewing supplies
- rotary cutter and mat (optional)
- quilter's ruler (optional)
- pressing cloth
- Contact paper
- template plastic
- fineline marker pen

Detail of Warm Hearts

A quilt book written by an Australian wouldn't be complete without a quilt made from wool. Growing up in an era when we lived 'off the sheeps' back' and our primary school years weren't complete without at least one project on wool, I feel we should explore the quilting possibilities of wool.

To overcome the problems of bumpy seams, designs with simple lines are necessary. Add the bold colours of wool and a stunning graphic quilt is the result.

Embellishing the crazy patchwork in feather stitch in gold thread is reminiscent of quilts of the Victorian era. The quilting design is an integral part of this quilt. Quilting in the same golden thread coordinates the quilting design with the rest of the quilt.

Machine-pieced and hand-quilted
Finished size: 33 cm (13 in) square

INSTRUCTIONS

See the Templates on page 58.
Note: The crazy blocks can be pieced by hand or on the machine.

1 Using the templates, cut four A squares from homespun or interfacing, adding a 6 mm (1/4 in) seam allowance all round.
2 Cut a scrap from the coloured wool, lay it in the centre of the calico (Fig. 1). Cut another scrap and lay it on top of the first with the right sides together. Sew them with a small seam allowance (Fig. 2). Fold the fabric back and press. It's a good idea to use a pressing cloth to prevent a shine from appearing on your work as there will be a large number of seams in a small area.
3 Continue adding pieces in this manner till the block is completed. Press and neaten the edges. Make four blocks.
4 Embroider with feather stitch over all the seams with two strands of Gold cotton.

TO FINISH

1 Make templates of the remaining pattern pieces B and C. Using these templates, cut four B and four C from black wool. Using template A, cut out the centre square from the black wool, remembering to add seam allowances.
2 Lay the blocks out, using figure 3 as a guide. Sew them together in diagonal rows, then sew the rows together.
3 Carefully press the quilt top, using a pressing cloth. Take care not to distort your work when pressing – be gentle, you're not doing the ironing!
4 Measure the length of the quilt and cut two 8 cm (3 in) wide strips the length of the quilt. Sew them to the sides of the quilt.
5 Measure the width of the quilt and cut two 8 cm (3 in) wide strips the width of the quilt. Sew them to the top and bottom of the quilt.
6 Lay the backing fabric down with the right side down. Lay the wadding down, with the quilt front on top, right side up. Pin and baste the three layers together.
7 Machine-quilt in the ditch round the crazy blocks and the border seams.
8 Embroider the feather stitch along the inner border seam in two strands of Gold embroidery cotton.
9 Trace the quilting pattern onto clear Contact paper and cut it out. Stick the hearts randomly on the quilt in a pleasing pattern. Quilt round the edge of the hearts, then remove the Contact paper. Randomly quilt a line which joins the hearts.
10 Bind the edges of the quilt, then complete the quilt with the feather stitch embroidery.

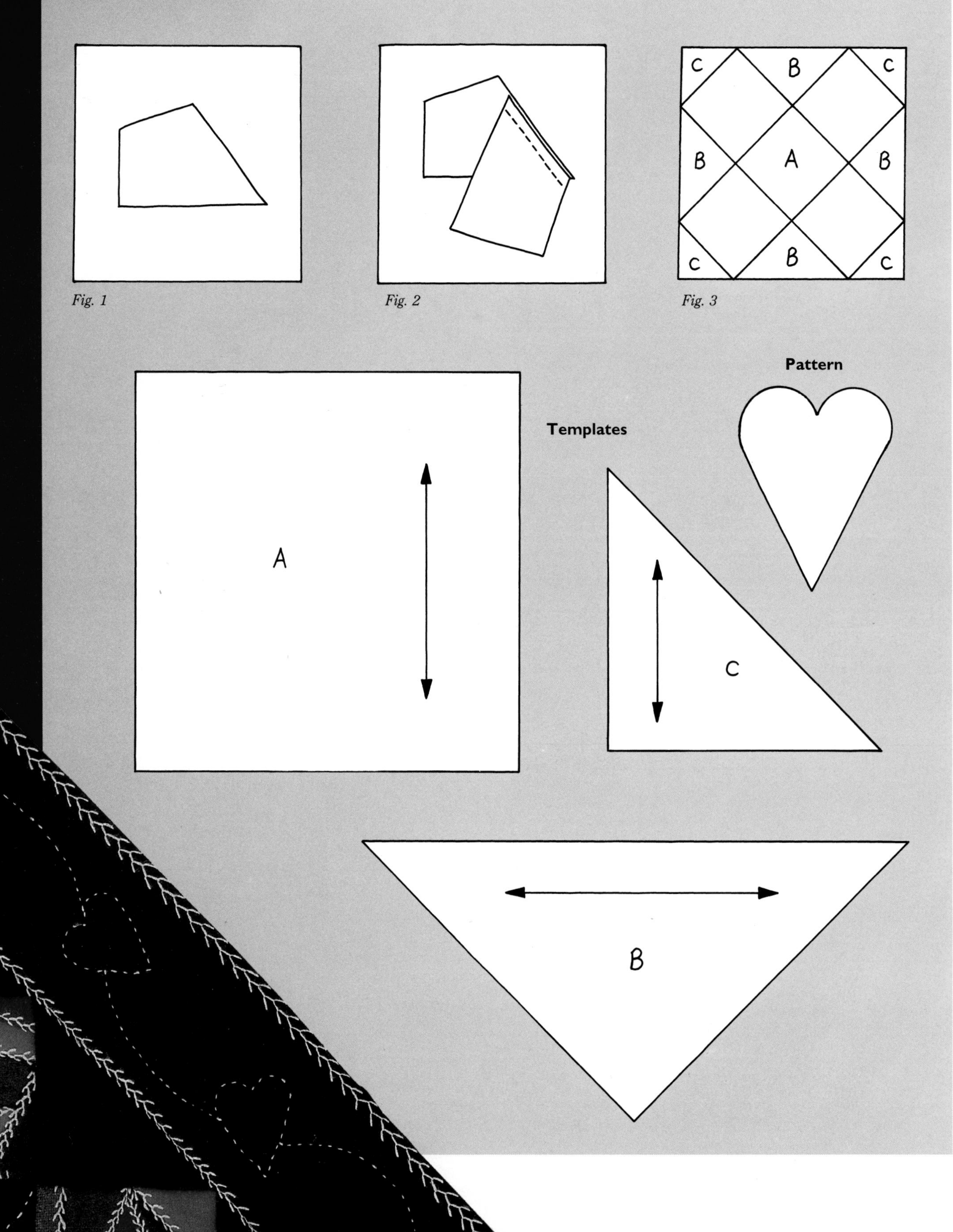

Fig. 1

Fig. 2

Fig. 3

Log Cabin Flying Geese

Log Cabin is perhaps the most frequently made quilting pattern. The simplicity of the design, the ease of making it and the variety of the finished quilts make it a most loved design. We all make a Log Cabin quilt in our lifetime, whether we need to make a quick quilt or one that best shows off the fabrics we've chosen, the reasons are many but the results are always pleasing.

Log Cabin Flying Geese is a variation on the original Log Cabin design where the small triangles running across the quilt add an extra dimension to the finished quilt. The variations allow us to create new designs within the original pattern or add extra colour and highlights.

Piecing this block with regular techniques can make it difficult to align the triangles accurately. However the pattern I have used is for the foundation piecing technique so your finished quilt will be accurate and straight. You may like to colour in your foundations to help guide your fabric layout as you are sewing.

The quilt is made with two alternating blocks. All the fabrics are the same for each block except for the last row which is alternated. This prevents you from ending up with the same two fabrics together, when the quilt is made up.

Machine-pieced on foundation
Finished size: 32 cm (12½ in) square
Block size: 5 cm (2 in) square

INSTRUCTIONS

See the Pattern on page 60.

For the Log Cabin Flying Geese blocks

1 Photocopy or trace the pattern onto the firm paper with the marker pen. Use this as your master copy. This allows you to use the pattern repeatedly without damaging your book.

2 Tape the tracing onto a firm surface, then tape the interfacing over the top and trace the pattern onto the interfacing with the marker pen. Remember that your finished block will only be as accurate as your tracing, so use a sharp pencil and trace accurately. Include the numbers, which indicate the sequence of sewing. You may also like to roughly colour in the interfacing to give you a guide as to the layout of the red and green fabrics. You will need sixteen blocks to complete the quilt.

3 Roughly cut the fabrics to the size of the finished piece, allowing 6 mm (¼ in) seam allowances. Set the stitch length on your machine to 5-6 stitches per centimetre (12-15 per inch) or approximately 1.5-2 stitch length and work with an open-toed or appliqué foot on your machine.

4 Starting with the centre square, lay a red fabric on the back of the interfacing with the right side out and covering the centre square, allowing a 6 mm (¼ in) seam allowance. Hold the piece up to the light and check that it is in the right position.

5 Lay a green fabric (piece 1) over the red centre square with the right sides together. Pin or hold the fabric in place. Turn the interfacing over and sew along the drawn line between the centre and piece1, starting three stitches before the line and finishing three stitches after it. This allows for the seam allowance. Carefully trim the seam if necessary and flip the green fabric over. Press.

YOU WILL NEED

Note: Fat quarters or 25 cm (10 in) squares of each fabric will provide an adequate quantity.

- four green fabrics for the Log Cabin
- four red fabrics for the Log Cabin
- red and green fabrics for the Flying Geese
- 10 cm (4 in) of red fabric for the inner border
- 20 cm (8 in) of fabric for the outer border and binding
- 40 cm (16 in) square of fabric for the backing
- 40 cm (16 in) square of wadding
- 20 cm (8 in) of medium-weight interfacing
- sewing machine
- sewing threads to blend with the fabrics
- rotary cutter, board and ruler (optional)
- firm white paper
- sharp pencil
- fineline marker pen
- usual sewing supplies
- masking tape
- pressing cloth

Detail of one block

6 Place the next green fabric (piece 2) down and sew, trim, flip and press, as before. Keep working in this manner, following the numbering sequence and changing the fabrics where necessary, till the block is finished. Press the block, then trim the edges, allowing 6 mm (¼ in) seam allowances on all sides of the block.

7 Sew the remaining blocks in the same way, remembering to change from red to green for some flying geese and alternating the outer fabric on each block.

8 Referring to figure 1, sew the blocks together in rows of four then sew the four rows together. Use a large stitch when sewing the blocks together, check that the pieces match, then oversew with a smaller stitch.

For the borders

Cut the inner border 2.5 cm x 35 cm (1 in x 14 in) and the outer border 6 cm x 35 cm (2½ in x 14 in). Sew them together and press the seams towards the outer border. Refer to the section on page 11 for how to sew borders.

TO FINISH

1 Lay the backing fabric down with the wrong side up. Lay the wadding down on it, then the pieced front on top of that, face upwards. Press the three layers together gently. Pin, then baste the layers together.

2 Quilt in a pattern of your choice. I have hand-quilted round the inner and outer borders. This is enough to hold the three layers together without distorting the tiny pieces in the quilt.

3 Bind and label your quilt.

Fig. 1

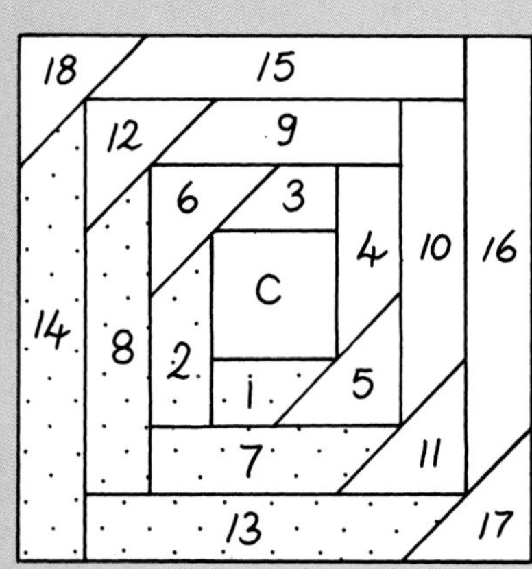

Pattern

Tumbling Blocks

YOU WILL NEED

- a variety of light, dark and medium (beige) fabrics
- 30 cm (12 in) of fabric for the border
- 39 cm x 46 cm (16 in x 18 in) of wadding
- 39 cm x 46 cm (16 in x 18 in) of fabric for the backing
- stranded embroidery cotton, Black
- template plastic
- fineline marker pen
- sharp pencil
- sandpaper
- usual sewing supplies
- sewing thread to blend with the fabric
- pressing cloth

Detail of the blocks

The three-dimensional surface created with the careful placement of light, medium and dark fabrics can be stark and graphic in plain fabrics, or as charming as naive patchwork in the soft fabrics that I have chosen. Choose your fabrics carefully, swapping with your friends for that special fabric you need. The greater the variety of scraps the more interest is created. Try making it a charm quilt where every fabric is different.

Hand-pieced and hand-quilted
Finished size: 39 cm x 46 cm (15 1/2 in x 18 in)

INSTRUCTIONS

See the Templates on page 64.

1 Trace the templates accurately onto the template plastic. Cut them out with sharp scissors. Check the template against the pattern for accuracy.
2 Lay the sandpaper under the fabric to keep the fabric from slipping while you mark it. Trace round the template on the wrong side of the fabric using the pencil.
3 Cut out the diamond shapes, leaving a small seam allowance.
4 Choose three diamonds – one each of light, beige and dark fabric – to sew a block. Note that the fabrics need to be in the same position in each block. Begin with the shorter seam by placing one medium and one dark fabric with the right sides together (Fig. 1). Place a pin through the fabrics, matching the end of the seam. Begin at the other end with a back stitch, then sew to the end on the pencil line (Fig. 1). Finish off the thread. Complete the block by adding the third diamond of beige fabric (Fig. 2). Sew forty-one large blocks using template A, ten small blocks using template E, six half-blocks using templates B and A and two fillers using template B (Fig. 3).

TO FINISH

1 Lay the segments out and experiment with the layout until you find one that pleases you. Sew the blocks into rows, using the half-blocks and fillers. Join the rows together, adding the small filler segments (B plus B) in the corners.
2 Add half-diamonds cut using template C from the border fabric, to the top and bottom of the quilt. This gives a straight edge to the quilt.
3 Using templates D1 and D2, cut one piece with each template, then turn the templates over and cut another piece. Join these pieces to the corners.
4 Measure the length of the quilt, then cut two 8 cm (3 1/4 in) wide strips the length of the quilt. Sew them to the sides of the quilt.
5 Measure the width of the quilt, then cut two 8 cm (3 1/4 in) wide strips the width of the quilt. Sew them to the top and bottom of the quilt (Fig. 4).
6 Work the decorative feather stitch in two strands of black cotton.
7 I have finished the edge of this quilt by taking the border fabric over to the back of the quilt and stitching it down. Press 6 mm (1/4 in) round the edges of the quilt onto the back. Press another fold 3 cm (1 1/4 in) from the previous one. Lay the quilt down with the backing facing upwards. Fold in the corners (Fig. 5). Slipstitch the pressed edges down, mitring the corners (Fig. 6).

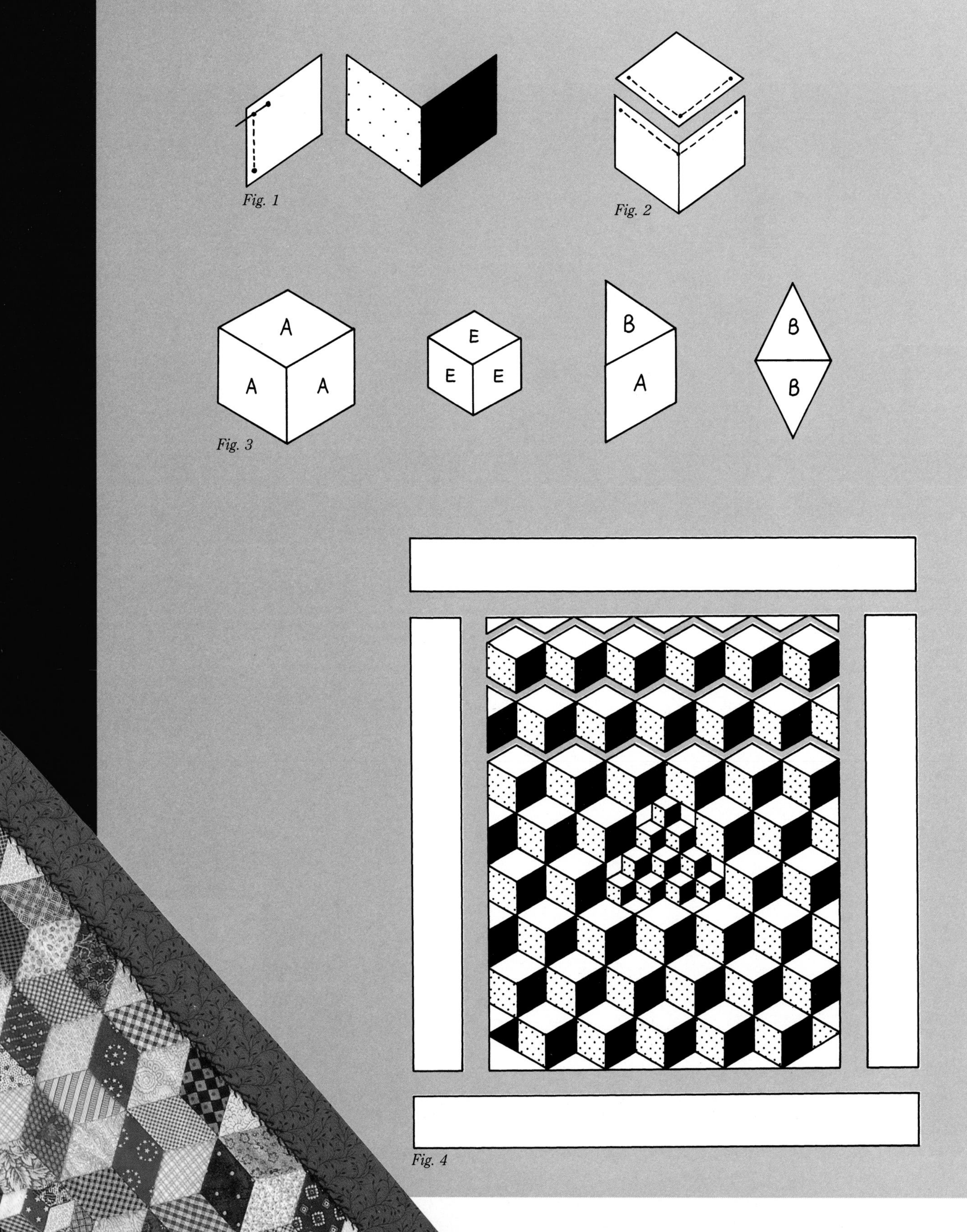

Fig. 1

Fig. 2

Fig. 3

Fig. 4

Fig. 5

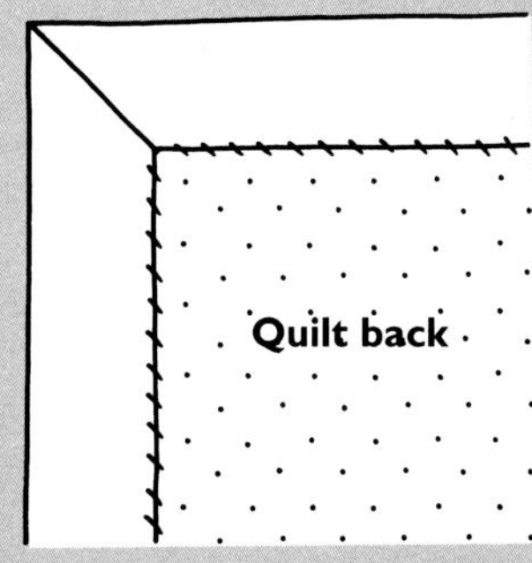

Fig. 6

Templates

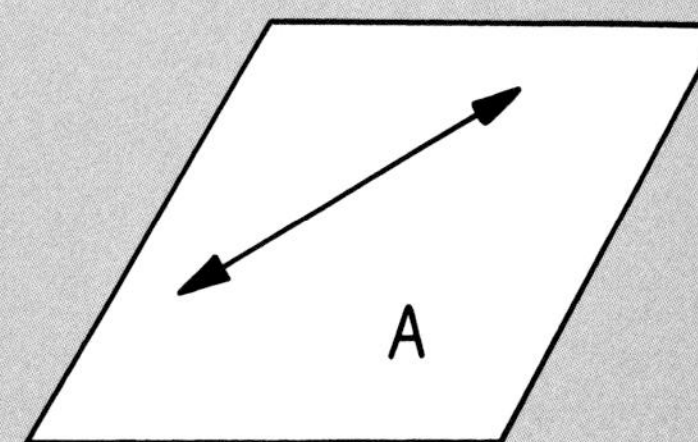

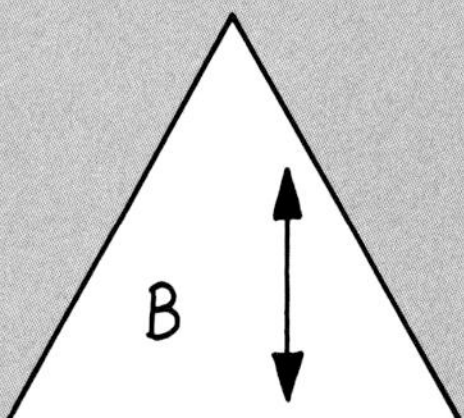

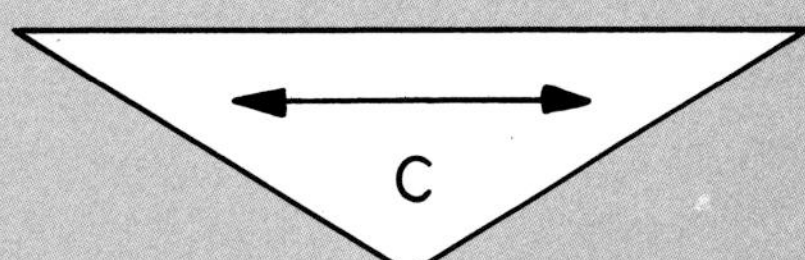

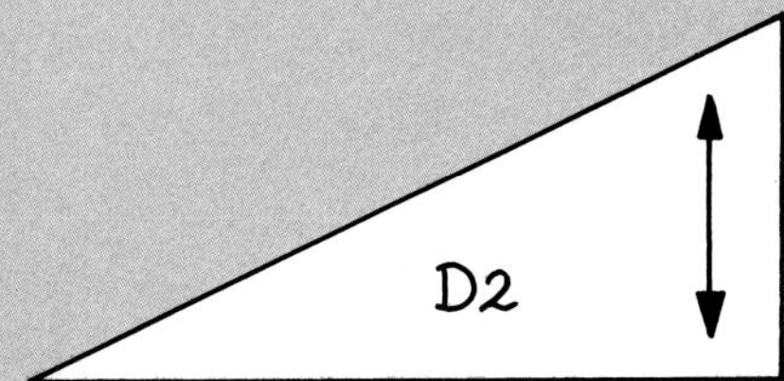

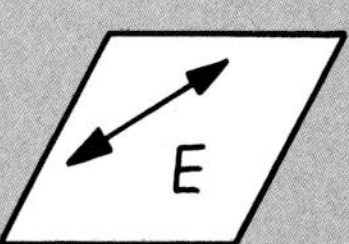

Grandmother's Treasures

YOU WILL NEED

- 30 cm (12 in) of fabric for the background
- coordinating scrap fabrics for the flowers, soft florals are best
- 30 cm (12 in) of white fabric
- template plastic
- sandpaper
- needle
- sewing thread to blend with the fabrics
- sharp pencil

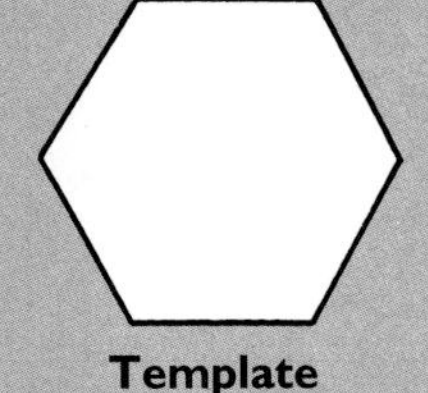

Template

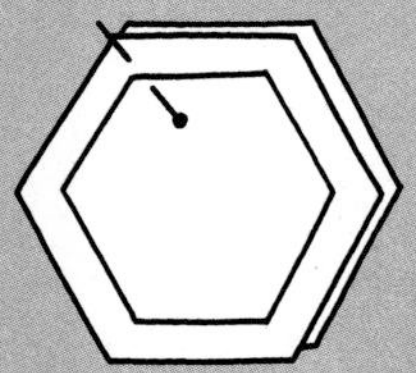

Fig. 1

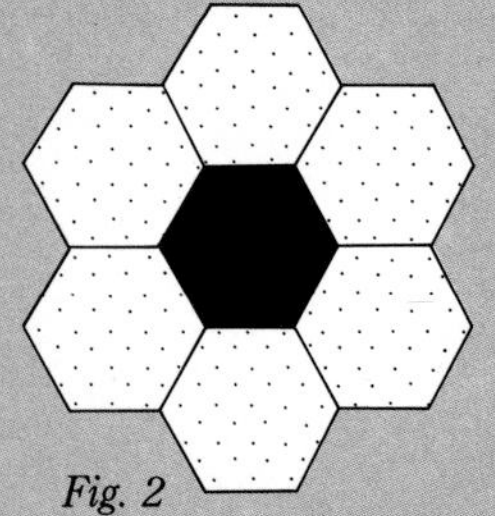

Fig. 2

Love them or hate them, hexagon quilts are evocative. Maybe your grandmother sewed hexagon quilts for the family or this was the start of your first quilt. Many a quilter has an unfinished hexagon quilt in the cupboard. Completing the tedious process of cutting papers, basting the fabric, then whip stitching the pieces together for a large quilt was beyond most of us.

Create your own piece of hexagon history – choose your oldest fabrics with the most memories and lovingly stitch your hexagon sampler together by hand. I have pieced this using the American piecing technique without papers and found it went together quickly and accurately.

Decorate the finished piece with a few miniature sewing tools and frame it to create your own family heirloom. This piece was not quilted and wadding was not added as it was being framed.

Hand-pieced and hand-quilted
Finished size: 21 cm x 28 cm ($8^1/2$ in x 11 in)
Hexagon size: 12 mm ($^1/2$ in)

INSTRUCTIONS

See the Template on this page.

For the hexagons

1 Lay the template plastic over the pattern and trace it accurately. Cut out the template with sharp scissors. Check the template against the pattern for accuracy.

2 Place the sandpaper under the fabric to keep the fabric from slipping while you mark it. Using a sharp pencil, trace round the template on the wrong side of the fabric.

3 Cut out the hexagon shapes, leaving a small seam allowance.

4 Place two pieces with the right sides together with a pin through the fabrics at the end of the row, matching the end of the seam (Fig. 1). Sewing on the pencil line, start at the other end with a back stitch and sew to the pinned end, then finish off the thread.

5 Place the next hexagon in position with the right sides together. Pin at the end of the row and sew on the line, as before.

6 Sew the required number of hexagon 'flowers' (Fig. 2).

TO FINISH

1 Using the quilt photograph as a guide, add the background hexagons to complete the quilt top.

2 Add 15 cm (6 in) strips of white fabric to the outer edge. This is needed for the framer to mount the piece. Don't forget to add those treasured keepsakes – a family thimble, scissors, tape measure or any special mementos that are in keeping.

Detail of a hexagon-flower

Storm in a Forest

YOU WILL NEED

- nine fat quarters or 30 cm (12 in) squares of fabric graduating through the range of a single colour
- 40 cm (16 in) of cream fabric for the background
- 20 cm (8 in) each of two fabrics for the borders and binding
- 42 cm x 47 cm (16$^1/_2$ in x 18$^1/_2$ in) of fabric for the backing
- 42 cm x 47 cm (16$^1/_2$ in x 18$^1/_2$ in) of wadding
- 30 cm (12 in) of medium-weight interfacing
- sewing machine
- usual sewing supplies
- sewing threads to blend with the fabrics
- rotary cutter and mat
- quilter's ruler
- sharp pencil
- fineline marker pen
- firm white paper
- masking tape
- small plastic bags
- pressing cloth

This little quilt is not for the faint-hearted – perseverance is required to finish it, but the results are worth it. This one was destined for the rubbish bin many a time, but my daughter kept at me and I'm thrilled with the finished piece.

While this Storm at Sea design is usually worked in blue scraps, my graduated green fabrics led to 'Storm in a Forest', which has a more contemporary feel. Some stores sell fabric that is printed with graduated colours on the one piece. If you are unable to find any of this fabric, collect nine fat quarters of fabric, from very dark to the palest shade.

The fabric placement may look complex, but a few simple steps will help. Lay the fabrics out in the order of the colour graduation. In one corner, number the fabrics from 1 to 9 (lightest to darkest). This is essential; as there is sometimes very little difference between two adjoining fabrics, it is easy to pick up the wrong one.

Follow the quilt diagram on page 70 for a guide to the fabric placement. Sew all the foundations with the lightest fabric and pin them to a cork board. Repeat, sewing all the foundations of one colour at a time. Note that some foundations will have a corner with a different fabric.

The pattern can be enlarged on the photocopier to a more manageable size, if you find the small size too difficult to sew.

Machine-pieced on foundation and machine-quilted
Finished size: 33 cm x 38 cm (13 in x 15 in)

INSTRUCTIONS

See the Pattern on page 70.

1. Photocopy or trace the pattern onto the firm paper with the marker pen. Use this as your master copy. This allows you to use the pattern repeatedly without damaging your book.
2. Tape the pattern onto a firm surface and trace the patterns onto the interfacing with the sharp pencil. Store them in small plastic bags as you work.
3. Piece the blocks, following the general instructions for foundation piecing on page 9. Make twenty A, forty-nine B and thirty C blocks. Press the finished blocks, then trim the edges, allowing a 6 mm ($^1/_4$ in) seam allowance on all sides.
4. Lay out the quilt, using the photograph and figure 1 as a guide. Join the blocks together into rows, then join the rows together. Remember to sew the rows together with a large stitch first, then oversew with a small stitch when all the points are accurately matched up.

TO FINISH

1. Cut one border 6 cm x 35 cm (2$^1/_2$ in x 14 in) and one 6 cm x 40 cm (2$^1/_2$ in x 16 in) each from a medium and a dark fabric. Add the borders, following the instructions for mitred borders on page 11.
2. Lay the backing fabric face down with the wadding on top and the quilt front on top of that, face upwards. Pin and baste the three layers together.
3. Machine-quilt in the ditch around the borders.
4. Bind and label your quilt.

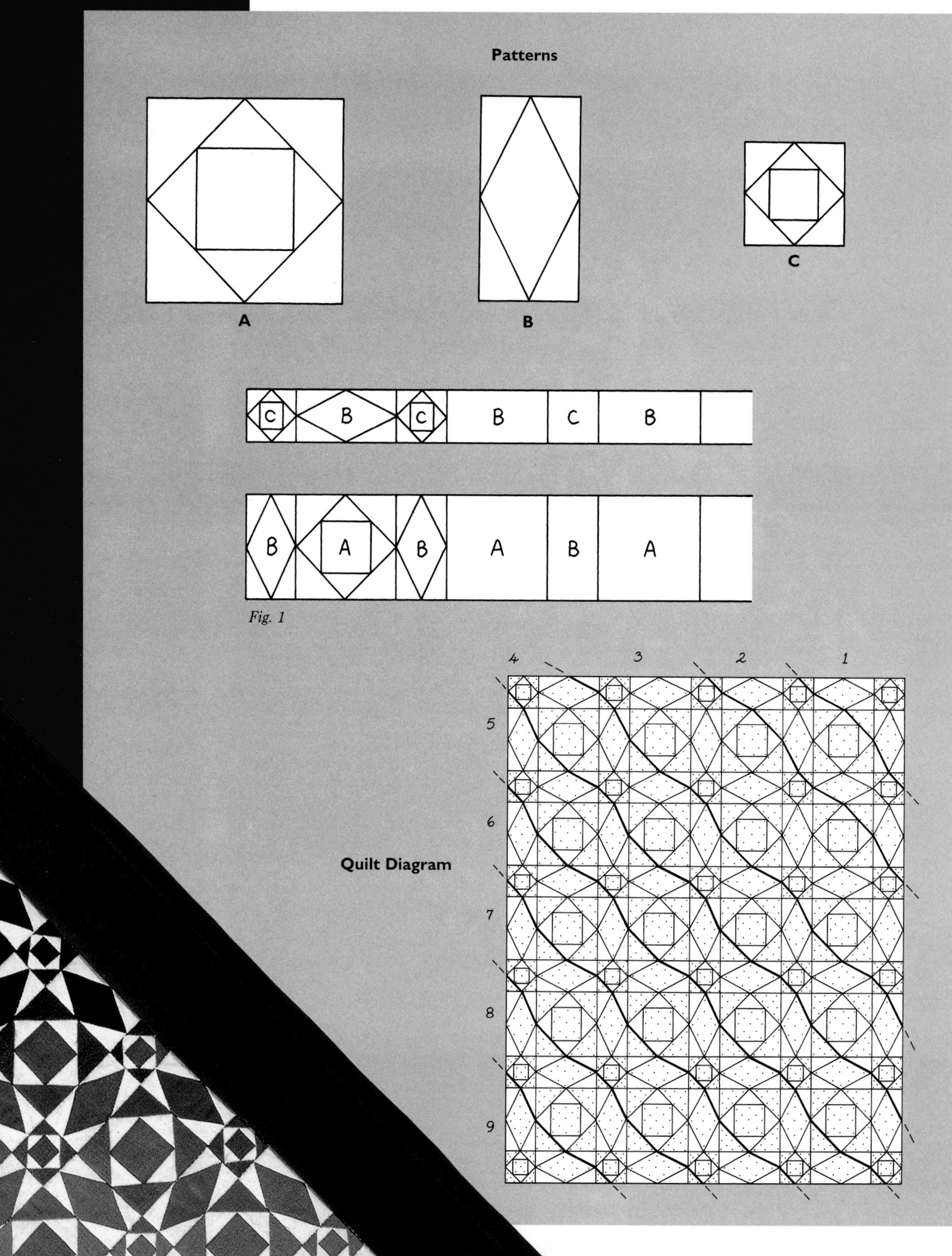

Fig. 1

Red Schoolhouse

This traditional pattern, which is always sewn in red and white or cream has been a favourite of mine for years, but as the colour scheme clashed with the colours in my home, I was hesitant to put hours of work into a full-sized quilt that wouldn't be used on a bed. The miniature size fulfils my creative urge to make a Schoolhouse quilt.

You can create your own look with this pattern. The options are endless. I've worked with five Schoolhouse blocks as I wanted to quilt in the alternate blocks, but you could have nine Schoolhouse blocks; work in Amish or country colours or add plain borders, if you prefer.

Machine-pieced on foundation and hand-quilted
Finished size: 39.5 cm (15½ in) square
Block size: 7.5 cm (3 in)

INSTRUCTIONS

See the Pattern and Template on page 72.

SCHOOLHOUSE BLOCK

For section 1

Note: The quilt is worked in the foundation technique. As the house block is more complex than other foundation work, three foundation sections are needed to make the block. Each section is sewn and trimmed, allowing a 6 mm (¼ in) seam allowance on all sides, then the three sections pieced together to finish the block.

1. Photocopy or trace the pattern onto the firm paper with the marker pen. Use this as your master copy. This allows you to use the pattern repeatedly without damaging your book. The image will be reversed when sewn.
2. Tape the tracing to a firm surface with the interfacing on top. Trace the pattern onto the interfacing, leaving 2.5 cm (1 in) between them. Be accurate and include the numbers which indicate the sequence of sewing. Shade the sections that will be red fabric as a guide to the layout when you begin sewing. Cut the three sections for each block apart.
3. Roughly cut the fabrics to the size of the finished pieces allowing 6 mm (¼ in) seam allowances.
4. Set the stitch length on your machine to 5-6 stitches per centimetre (12-15 stitches per inch) or approximately 1.5 stitch length and work with an open-toed or appliqué foot. Starting with section 1 and piece 1, lay a piece of red fabric in position on the back of the interfacing, allowing a 6 mm (¼ in) seam allowance. Pin or hold it in place. Hold the interfacing up to the light to check that piece 1 is in the correct position, then place the piece 2 fabric (white or cream) over it. Hold the fabric in place, turn the interfacing over and sew along the drawn line between pieces 1 and 2, starting three stitches before the line and finishing three stitches after. This allows for the seam allowance. Carefully trim the seam allowance, flip piece 2 over and press. Place piece 3 fabric down and sew, trim, flip and press, as before. Keep working in this manner till piece 9 is sewn in place.
5. Piece 10 is made of two fabrics which need to be joined before sewing them onto the foundation. Sew a red and a white (or cream) fabric together and press. Check that the seam line matches the line on the foundation, then proceed as previously.
6. Press the finished section of the block and trim with the rotary cutter, allowing a 6 mm (¼ in) seam allowance on all sides of the section.

For section 2

Sew in the same manner as for section 1.

YOU WILL NEED

- 20 cm (8 in) of white or cream homespun for the Schoolhouse blocks, alternating blocks and border
- 40 cm (16 in) of red homespun for the Schoolhouse blocks, borders and binding
- 50 cm (20 in) square of wadding
- 50 cm (20 in) square of fabric for the backing
- 20 cm (8 in) of medium-weight, sew-in interfacing
- sharp pencil
- rotary cutter and mat
- quilter's ruler
- usual sewing supplies
- sewing thread to blend with the fabric
- firm white paper
- fineline marker pen
- pressing cloth
- Contact paper
- masking tape

Detail of one Schoolhouse block

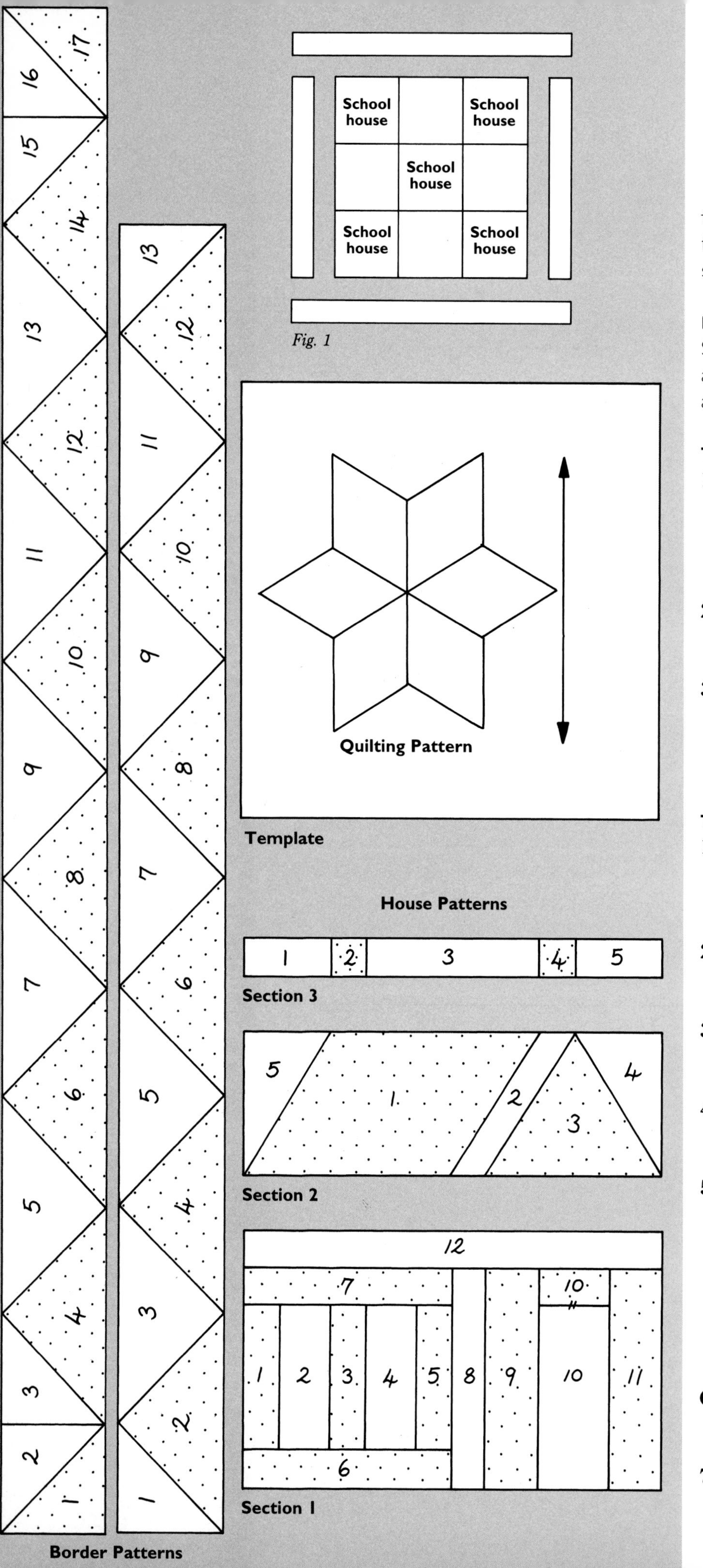

Fig. 1

I find it easier to start with the roof section, then add the other fabrics. Trim around the finished section allowing a 6 mm (1/4 in) seam allowance.

For section 3

Sew this section the same as for sections 1 and 2. Trim around the finished section allowing a 6 mm (1/4 in) seam allowance.

To assemble the blocks

1. Lay out the three sections then sew them together. Sew with a large stitch first, check that the points match, then oversew with a smaller stitch. Complete all the blocks in the same manner.
2. Using template A, cut out four white or cream blocks, adding 6 mm (1/4 in) seam allowances.
3. Using the photograph as a guide, lay out the completed pieced blocks and the alternating white or cream blocks. Join them into three rows of three blocks.

TO FINISH

1. Trace the inner border strips onto the interfacing and sew them in the same manner as the blocks. The shaded parts on the pattern indicate the red fabric.
2. Join the inner border strips to the sides first, then to the top and bottom of the quilt top (Fig. 1).
3. Cut the red fabric borders 5 cm (2 in) wide and sew them to the quilt in the same way as the inner borders.
4. Lay the backing fabric down, wrong side up, then the wadding and the quilt top, right side up. Baste the layers together.
5. Trace the star quilting design onto Contact paper. Cut it out and stick one on each white or cream block. Quilt round the edge of the star, remove the template, then fill in the centre lines of the design. This is a great idea for quilting shapes and saves the worry of removing marking lines later.
6. Lay masking tape on the quilt as a guide for the cross-hatched quilting design in the red border.
7. Bind and label your quilt.

Snail's Trail

YOU WILL NEED

- 30 cm (12 in) each of light and dark fabrics (for a scrap version: twenty-four 15 cm (6 in) squares each of light and dark fabrics)
- 30 cm (12 in) of fabric for the borders and binding
- 40 cm x 50 cm (16 in x 20 in) of wadding
- 40 cm x 50 cm (16 in x 20 in) of fabric for the backing
- 20 cm (8 in) medium-weight interfacing
- sewing machine
- sewing threads that blend with the fabrics
- rotary cutter and mat (optional)
- quilter's ruler (optional)
- usual sewing supplies
- masking tape
- sharp pencil
- firm white paper
- fineline marker pen
- pressing cloth

Contemporary or traditional? I love the way the old traditional patterns lend themselves to a contemporary look with just a change in fabrics and layout. An unusual silk fabric gave the creative look to my contemporary version. Light on one side and dark on the other, with a hand-dyed look, it was exciting to see the colours come together as I randomly pieced the blocks. Country-style fabrics will give this quilt the traditional look that most people recognise as Snail's Trail. A bag of scraps of light and dark fabrics and a few hours sewing time are all that's needed to make your traditional quilt.

Machine-pieced on foundation and machine-quilted
Finished size: 37 cm x 44 cm (14½ in x 17½ in)
Block size: 7.5 cm (3 in)

INSTRUCTIONS

See the Pattern on page 77.

1 Photocopy or trace the pattern onto the firm paper with the marker pen. Use this as your master copy. This allows you to use the pattern repeatedly without damaging your book.

Detail of the block

2 Tape the master copy onto a firm surface, then tape the interfacing over the top and trace the pattern onto the interfacing. Remember that your finished block will only be as accurate as your tracing so use a sharp pencil and trace accurately. Include the numbers, which indicate the sequence of sewing. You will need twelve blocks for the quilt.

For the blocks

1 Make the Four-patch section first. Cut two 2.5 cm (1 in) wide strips of fabric, one light and one dark. Sew them together and press the seam to the dark side. Cut the strip into 2.5 cm (1 in) segments and sew them into a Four-patch (Figs 1 and 2). This is larger than needed; it will be trimmed later.

2 Lay the Four-patch in the centre of the interfacing pattern, on the wrong side with the fabric right side out. Line up the dark and light patches with the appropriate square on the interfacing.

3 Roughly cut out a dark triangle (number 1 on the pattern), allowing 6 mm (¼ in) seam allowances. Lay it over the Four-patch and pin it in place. Turn the interfacing over and sew on the line between the Four-patch and piece 1, starting three stitches before the line and finishing three stitches after the line to allow for seam allowances. Carefully trim the seam if necessary and flip the dark fabric over, then press (Fig. 3).

4 Place the number 2 fabric (a dark triangle) down, and sew, trim, flip and press as before (Fig. 4). Keep working in this manner, following the numbering sequence and remembering to alternate the light and dark fabrics till the block is finished.

ARTIST'S
ACRYLIC
COLOUR
Violet Prisme
Prismaviolett
Violeta Prisma
60ml ℮ 2 US fl oz
Prism Violet
Oil Colors
VIOLET

5 Press the block then trim the edges with a rotary cutter allowing 6 mm (1/4 in) seam allowances on all sides of the block.

6 Sew the remaining blocks in the same manner.

TO FINISH

1 Using the quilt photograph as a guide, sew the blocks together into four rows of three blocks, then sew the rows together. Use a large stitch when sewing the blocks together, check that the pieces match, then oversew with a smaller stitch.

2 Measure the length of the quilt and cut two 4 cm (1 1/2 in) wide strips the length of the quilt for the side borders. Sew them to the sides of the quilt.

3 Measure the width of the quilt and cut two 4 cm (1 1/2 in) wide strips the width of the quilt. Sew them to the top and bottom of the quilt.

4 Lay the quilt on the cutting board aligning it with the lines on the board. Decide on the degree of angle you want and move the quilt accordingly. Using the lines on the board, cut the outer borders at the appropriate angle (Fig. 5).

5 Lay the backing fabric down with the wrong side up. Place the wadding on top, then lay the quilt on top, face up. Pin and baste the three layers together.

6 Quilt by hand or machine. I have only quilted parallel lines in the outer borders.

7 Bind the quilt and remember to add the label on the back.

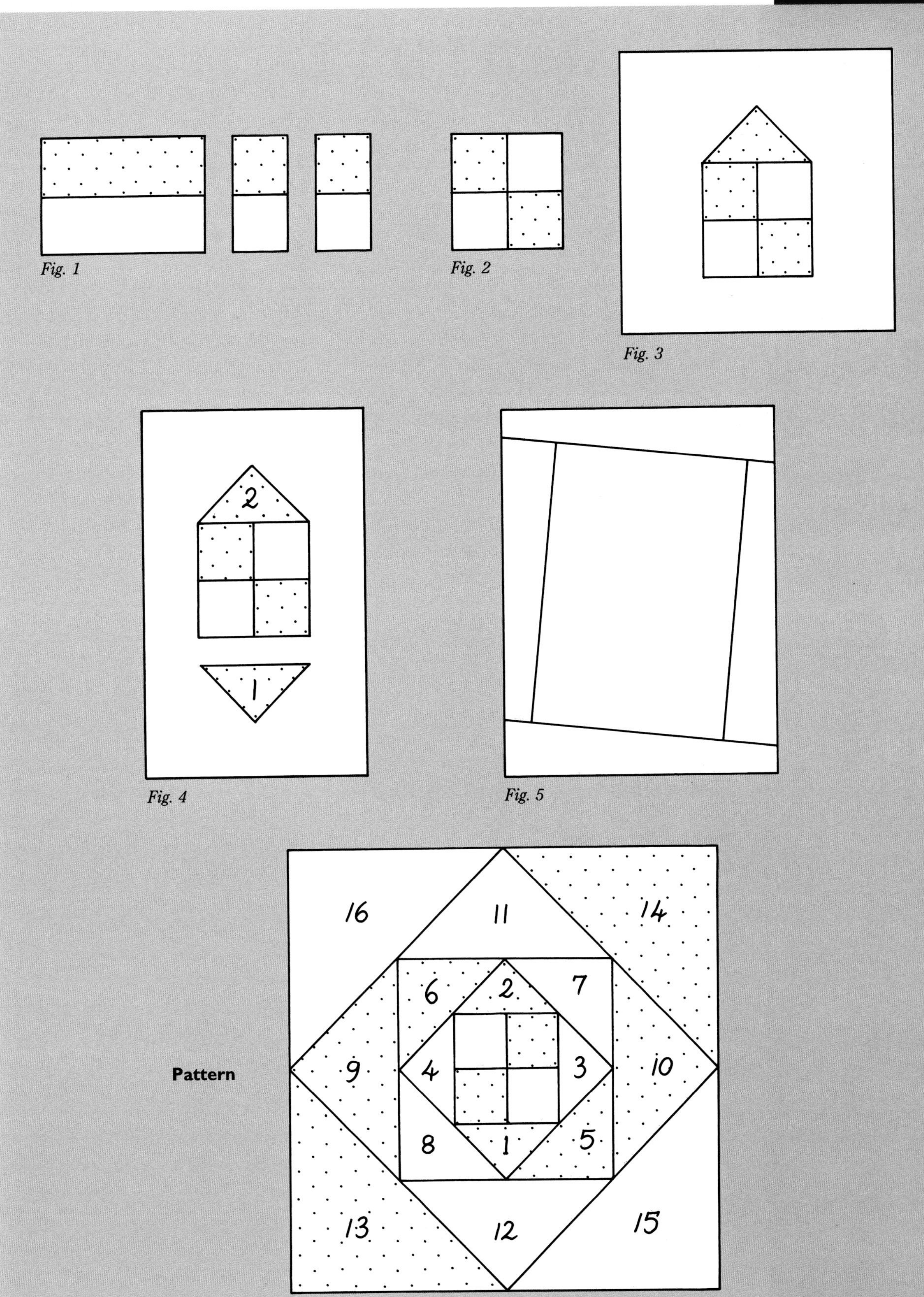

Fig. 1

Fig. 2

Fig. 3

Fig. 4

Fig. 5

Pattern

Miniature Colourwash

YOU WILL NEED

- 25 cm (10 in) squares of approximately thirty fabrics, ranging from light to dark
- 45 cm (18 in) square of thin wadding
- 45 cm (18 in) square of fabric for the backing
- 20 cm (8 in) of fabric for the binding
- iron-on interfacing
- monofilament thread
- sewing threads to blend with the fabrics
- usual sewing supplies
- sheet of GLAD Bake or greaseproof paper
- rotary cutter and mat
- quilter's ruler
- pencil

The flow of colour blending across this quilt in a painterly effect is reminiscent of the work of the Impressionists. Many quilters work in this colourwash style, creating large quilts and wallhangings. My colourwash quilts have been influenced by the work of Judy Turner, a prolific Australian quiltmaker, tutor and author. This particular miniature quilt was also influenced by the work of Deidre Amsden.

Initially, I felt it would be too difficult to sew hundreds of tiny pieces together accurately to achieve the colourwash effect, so I adapted a technique commonly used by embroiderers and I'm thrilled with the result.

Choose your fabrics carefully, taking the time to play around with them.

Machine-pieced and machine-quilted
Finished size: 41 cm (16 in) square

INSTRUCTIONS

Note: Lay all the fabrics out in a row, ranging from light to dark, before you begin. Try to keep a balance when laying out the fabrics. The centre square has a very small amount of very dark and very light fabrics. As you work out towards the strips, larger amounts of light and dark fabrics will be used.

1 The pattern pieces are as follows: piece 1 is 15 cm (6 in) square, piece 2 is 6 cm x 15 cm (2 1/2 in x 6 in), piece 3 is 6 cm x 21 cm (2 1/2 in x 8 1/2 in), piece 4 is 6 cm x 21 cm (2 1/2 in x 8 1/2 in), piece 5 is 6 cm x 27 cm (2 1/2 in x 11 in), piece 6 is 6 cm x 27 cm (2 1/2 in x 11 in), piece 7 is 6 cm x 33 cm (2 1/2 in x 13 1/2 in), piece 8 is 6 cm x 33 cm (2 1/2 in x 13 1/2 in), piece 9 is 6 cm x 39 cm (2 1/2 in x 16 in).

Cut squares and strips from the iron-on interfacing that are 2.5 cm (1 in) larger than the sizes given above. For the centre square, draw a pencil line diagonally through the centre. This line will be your placement guide for the placement of the light to dark fabrics. When you are placing the fabrics, you should have reached the middle of your light to dark range of fabrics.

2 Cut 5 cm (2 in) squares from the four lightest fabrics. Cut these fabrics into 6 mm (1/4 in) squares. Using the photograph as a guide, place these squares at random on the adhesive side of the centre piece of interfacing where the fabrics will be the lightest.

3 Repeat step 2 with the next lightest four fabrics. If the contrast between the two groups is too great when they are laid down, move some of the pieces around a little to blend the two groups together.

4 Continue working in this manner until the whole piece of interfacing is covered. Place a sheet of GLAD Bake or greaseproof paper over the piece and press gently with the iron.

5 Randomly sew over the piece, using free-machine stitching. To do this, attach a darning foot to your machine, drop the feed dogs and thread the machine with monofilament thread. To work this sewing most effectively, imagine you are scribbling on the surface and the needle is your pencil. Hold the piece carefully, with the fabric pieces on top, sewing at top speed and moving the piece around slowly. It might be useful to practise this technique on scraps before you begin work on your quilt. The piece is quite

delicate until this sewing is completed, so handle it with care.

Note: Some sewing machines manage this type of sewing without lowering the feed dogs. Before you begin sewing, read the manufacturer's manual for your particular machine and do a sample piece.

6 Cut out the centre square, using the (1/4 in) seam allowance all the way around.

7 Cut and make up pieces 2 to 5 in the same manner, remembering to add the 6 mm (1/4 in) seam allowance when you cut them out (Fig. 1).

8 Sew pieces 2, 3, 4, and 5 around the centre square, following figure 1.

9 Cut and make up pieces 6 to 9 in the same manner as before. Join them to the centre section, following figure 2. Take care to place the light and dark sections in the correct places.

TO FINISH

1 Lay the backing fabric down, wrong side up, with the wadding on top and the quilt front on top of that, right side up. Pin and baste the three layers together.

2 Machine-quilt in the ditch around the seam lines.

3 Bind and label your quilt.

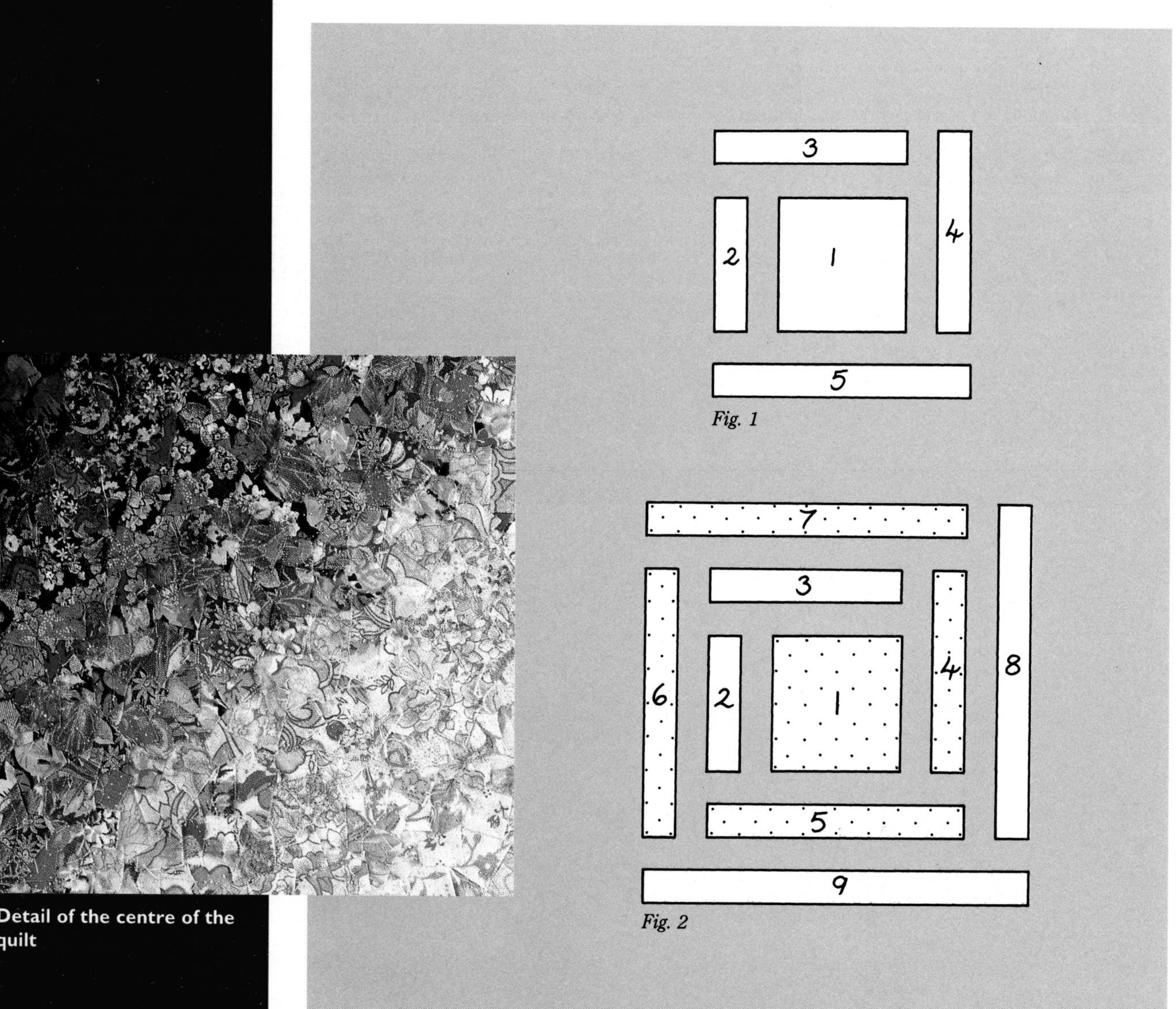

Fig. 1

Fig. 2

Detail of the centre of the quilt